Broadman Comments

April–June, 1992

on
THE INTERNATIONAL BIBLE LESSONS

for
Christian Teaching

CONVENTION UNIFORM SERIES

Volume 47   Number 3

BROADMAN PRESS
NASHVILLE, TENNESSEE

This material was first published in
Broadman Comments, 1991–92.
© Copyright 1991 • Broadman Press
Nashville, Tennessee
All rights reserved

4215-90
ISBN: 0-8054-1590-4

Broadman Comments is published quarterly by Broadman Press,
127 Ninth Avenue, North, Nashville, Tennessee 37234.
When ordered with other church literature, it sells for $3.50 per quarter.
Second-class postage paid at Nashville Tennessee.

ISSN 0068-2721

The Outlines of the International Sunday School Lessons,
Uniform Series, are copyrighted by the Committee on the
Uniform Series and are used by permission.

POSTMASTER: Send address change to *Broadman Comments*,
Customer Service Center, 127 Ninth Avenue, North
Nashville, Tennessee 37234

Dewey Decimal Classification 268.61
Printed in the United States of America

Broadman Comments
April–June

Writers

Studying the Bible
Donald F. Ackland has written the biblical interpretation portion of *Broadman Comments* since 1970.

Applying the Lesson
Brian L. Harbour is a pastor in Richardson, Texas.

Teaching the Class
Polly Cooper is a psychologist, Counseling and Development Center, Dallas, Texas. She has been writing teaching procedures for adults since 1972.

Contents

The Strong Son of God

Apr.	5	Love Says It All	9
Apr.	12	The Crucified Son of God	17
Apr.	19	An Empty Tomb	24

God's People in the World

Apr.	26	The Gift of Living Hope	33
May	3	Called to Be God's People	40
May	10	Witness in the Midst of Suffering	47
May	17	Humble, Steadfast, Vigilant	55
May	24	Growing in Grace	62
May	31	Focused on the Future	70

God's Judgment and Mercy

June	7	The Lord Will Restore Judah	79
June	14	Fleeing From God	86
June	21	Jonah Sulks, and God Saves	94
June	28	Judgment and Salvation	102

Abbreviations and Translations

GNB	From the *Good News Bible*, The Bible in Today's English Version. Old Testament: Copyright © American Bible Society, 1976; New Testament: Copyright © American Bible Society, 1966, 1971, 1976. Used by permission.
KJV	*King James Version*
NASB	From the *New American Standard Bible*. © The Lockman Foundation, 1960, 1962, 1963, 1968, 1971, 1972, 1973, 1975, 1977. Used by permission.
NIV	From the Holy Bible, *New International Version*, copyright © 1973, 1978, 1984 by International Bible Society. Used by permission.
NRSV	From the *New Revised Standard Version Bible* copyright © 1989, by the Division of Christian Education of the National Council of Churches of Christ in the United States of America, and used by permission.
RSV	From the *Revised Standard Version of the Bible* copyright 1946, 1952, © 1971, 1973 by the National Council of the Churches of Christ in the U.S.A., and used by permission.
TLB	Verses marked TLB are taken from *The Living Bible*. Copyright © Tyndale House Publishers, Wheaton, Illinois, 1971. Used by permission.

April 5

Love Says It All

Basic Passages: Deuteronomy 6:4-9; Mark 12:28-37

Focal Passage: Mark 12:28-37

We have entered April, and we are fast approaching the celebration of Easter. For us, the season is one of brightness and joy, for spring has come, and nature is putting on its summer finery. Moreover, as Christians, we have seen beyond the cross to the empty tomb, and perhaps we have allowed the glory of the resurrection to exclude from our minds the agony of the crucifixion. The full gospel is that "Christ died for our sins . . . that he was buried, and that he rose again" (1 Cor. 15:3-4). In his Gospel, Mark allows us to walk the weary road with our Lord that brought Him to Jerusalem, accusation, condemnation, and death. The motivating power that enabled Him to face the pain and suffering that lay ahead was love, love for sinners, love for you and me. Not surprisingly, He taught the duty of love to God, but what is surprising is that He did this in an atmosphere of hate. He enables us to understand that love is victorious over all that opposes it, and that love of God and for God are the most powerful forces in the universe.

Study Aim: *To recognize the compulsion of love in our Lords' life and respond in love toward Him and others for His sake*

STUDYING THE BIBLE

Jesus had named Jerusalem as the scene of His coming humiliation and death. Yet here He was in that city, to which He had been making voluntary pilgrimage for many days (Mark 11:1,15). That this had been a painful journey, both for Him and His disciples, is made clear. "They were in the way going up to Jerusalem; and Jesus went before them: and they were amazed; and as they followed, they were afraid" (10:32). There is Jesus striding toward a cruel fate and His disciples fearfully sensing His determination, yet following in His steps as Jerusalem loomed nearer by every mile they trod.

I. Traps Set for Jesus

The theme of love, which we are to develop, must be given its true setting. Arrival in Jerusalem brought Jesus into almost immediate conflict with the ruling authorities, "the chief priests, and the scribes, and the elders" (11:27). After His cleansing of the temple, these people "sought how they might destroy him" (v. 18). His teaching was as offensive to them as His deeds, for after He had told a parable "they sought to lay hold on him" (12:12).

1. Tribute money (vv. 13-17).—Our Lord's enemies were smart in their scheming. They sought to create friction between Him and the Roman authorities by asking a question about the payment of taxes. His answer so skillfully evaded the issue, while at the same time teaching an important lesson, that His very enemies "marveled at him."

2. Resurrection relationships (vv. 18-27).—The political trap having failed, another group, Sadducees this time, tried to embarrass Jesus with a theological question. These people did not believe in resurrection, and their question was intended to ridicule the idea. Again Jesus silenced them by a reply from the Old Testament, which He accused them of not understanding.

II. A Sincere Inquirer (Mark 12:28-34)

In the crowd that had been listening to these exchanges between our Lord and His enemies was a scribe who was favorably impressed with His replies. As a scribe, he was considered an expert in the law of

Moses and an interpreter of the Old Testament Scriptures in general. Though scribes had begun as copiers of the ancient holy documents, they had advanced to being trusted authorities. This man stood in refreshing contrast to the majority of his colleagues and furnishes an example of the mistake of condemning people by their associations.

> 28 And one of the scribes came, and having heard them reasoning together, and perceiving that he had answered them well, asked him, Which is the first commandment of all?
> 29 And Jesus answered him, The first of all the commandments is, Hear, O Israel; The Lord our God is one Lord:
> 30 And thou shalt love the Lord thy God with all thy heart, and with all thy soul, and with all thy mind, and with all thy strength: this is the first commandment.
> 31 And the second is like, namely this, Thou shalt love thy neighbor as thyself. There is none other commandment greater than these.
> 32 And the scribe said unto him, Well, Master, thou hast said the truth: for there is one God; and there is none other but he:
> 33 And to love him with all the heart, and with all the understanding, and with all the soul, and with all the strength, and to love his neighbor as himself, is more than all whole burnt offerings and sacrifices.
> 34 And when Jesus saw that he answered discreetly, he said unto him, Thou art not far from the kingdom of God. And no man after that durst ask him any question.

1. The first commandment (28-30).—Our basic passages for this lesson include Deuteronomy 6:4-9, the opening words of which Jesus quoted in verse 29. "The Jews call these verses from Deuteronomy the *Shema*, from the Hebrew of the word, 'Hear.' No passage of the Old Testament is more important to them. It is the first portion to be committed to memory by a Jewish child. Every synagogue service is opened by its recital. Jewish rabbinical law requires that it be repeated twice daily by the faithful. All Jews accept it as the supreme confession of their faith."[1] The recital of "heart, . . . understanding, . . . soul, . . . strength" indicate that the total person must be involved in love for God. No department of life can be omitted, for there can be no partial loyalties.

2. Love's necessity (v. 31).—The second commandment may be found in Leviticus 19:18. It is expounded throughout the Old Testament in the utterances of many prophets who made clear that professed devotion to God is valueless unless accompanied by just and compassionate treatment of others. Our Lord's parable of the good Samaritan (Luke 10:25-37) was given to correct prevailing narrow definitions as to who constitutes a neighbor. Anyone in need, whom we can help, is our neighbor.

3. Our Lord's commendation (v. 34a).—The scribe's reply was remarkable for its spiritual insight. He not only accepted our Lord's answer to his question, but he affirmed the superiority of love over ritual sacrifices (v. 33). He thus took his stand with the most revolutionary teaching of the prophets (Mic. 6:6-8) and anticipated such New Testament teaching as Hebrews 10:1-6. Our Lord saw this scribe as ready to enter God's kingdom since he had already accepted divinely revealed truth.

4. Critics silenced (v. 34b).—For the time being, our Lord's handling of His critics and the gracious response to this scribe ended the dialogue between Him and His enemies. These realized they could not gain any advantage in a battle of words. Unfortunately, they resorted to other means to achieve their goal of destroying Jesus (11:18).

III. Jesus Asks a Question (Mark 12:35-37)

Although we have no information on the circumstances that gave rise to our Lord's question, the occasion throws light upon it. The Passover season brought Jews from all parts of Palestine to Jerusalem where they met in great patriotic fervor. Hopes ran high that this festive season would bring with it the manifestation of the messiah, as seen in the cries of the crowd when Jesus rode into the holy city: "Blessed is he that cometh in the name of the Lord: Blessed be the kingdom of our father David, that cometh in the name of the Lord: Hosanna in the highest" (11:9-10). The expected messiah was figured as a heroic deliverer who would overcome Israel's foes and reestablish the nation in its former glory, as, for example, in David's time.

> 35 And Jesus answered and said, while he taught in the temple, How say the scribes that Christ is the son of David?
> 36 For David himself said by the Holy Ghost, The Lord said to my Lord, Sit thou on my right hand, till I make thine enemies thy footstool.
> 37 David therefore himself calleth him Lord; and whence is he then his son? And the common people heard him gladly.

1. Son of David (v. 35).—Passages such as Psalm 2 and Isaiah 9:6-7 supported teaching that the coming messiah would be a descendant of David, the warrior king. This colored the supposed nature of the messiah ("the son of David") who, as David had conquered his enemies and enlarged the borders of Israel, would bear arms against the Romans and bring freedom and prestige to the nation. This, of course, was a dangerous as well as an erroneous concept. At feast time, with

Jerusalem crowded with pilgrims, it could lead to outbursts of patriotic zeal that would bring drastic reaction from the Romans who watched over proceedings in the temple from a fortress called Antonia. For this reason, and for the sake of His true mission, our Lord saw the importance of straightening out this popular idea.

2. Son of God (vv. 36-37a).—Quoting Psalm 110:1, Jesus asked why David referred to the messiah as "Lord" if he was to be David's son. Presumably, we have in these verses only the heart of our Lord's statement, but enough is here to make His purpose clear. He was repudiating the idea of the Messiah as only a human descendant of David and affirming His superior relationship and dignity. He is David's Lord, and, therefore, in the light of other New Testament teaching, Son of God as well as son of David. His mission, also, must be understood in the light of His divine sonship, for, as He said to Pilate, "My kingdom is not of this world" (John 18:36).

3. Popular reaction (v. 37b).—The "common people," ordinary folk as distinct from the religious leadership, responded enthusiastically to these dialogues between our Lord and their supposed spiritual superiors. No love was lost between the religious upper crust and the rank and file, for the Pharisees in particular imposed the rigorous rules and regulations that went far beyond the requirements of the Mosaic law. The question of 12:28 should be understood in light of the 613 commandments to which the basic law had been expanded. Those who bore the burden of these multiplied do's and don'ts rejoiced to see the humiliation of those who enforced them. But also there was admiration here for Jesus and a message to the believers of Rome, most of whom were "common people."

APPLYING THE LESSON

What to do with fear.—Fear is common to every life. What can we do about our fear? Step one is to clarify our fear. Sometimes, when we look closely at our fear we discover that the problem is not as great as we first supposed. On other occasions, we do discover a genuine problem which is the basis of our fear. In either case, clarifying our fear is the first step in dealing with it. The second step is then to confront our fear. An old English proverb suggests: "Fear knocked at the door; faith answered; and nobody was there."

With the eyes open.—A little boy had some puppies for sale. He had them in a box beside the road with a sign that said, "Puppies for sale. Only $5 each." Only one man stopped to investigate. After looking them over, he decided not to buy one. About a week later, this man passed by again and saw that the boy still had his puppies for sale. However, the price had changed. The sign now stated that the puppies cost $15 each. Curious at the change of price, the man stopped to talk to the boy. "Why do the puppies cost more now?" he asked the young entrepreneur. The young boy replied, "Look, Mister, they have their eyes open now, and that makes them worth a lot more!"

The boy spoke with more wisdom than he even knew. When we have our eyes open, we are worth more. No one was ever quite as alert and aware of what was going on as was Jesus. When His enemies attempted to trap Him, He had his eyes wide open.

True commitment.—Examples of true commitment can be found throughout Christian history. Colonial preacher Jonathan Edwards (1703-1758) was a man of commitment. Before he was nineteen, he wrote seventy resolutions in a diary that he kept religiously. Among those was the following: "Resolved: That every man should live to the glory of God. Resolved Second: That whether others do this or not, I will." Pioneer missionary William Carey (1761-1834) was another man of commitment. He expressed his faith in these words: "I am not my own, nor would I choose for myself. Let God employ me where he thinks fit." Dwight L. Moody (1837-1899), dynamic evangelist of the last century, was a man of commitment. After a sermon, one of his critics pointed out, "Mr. Moody, you made eleven mistakes in grammar in your message tonight." He responded, "That may be, but I'm using all the grammar I know in the service of Christ." F. B. Meyer (1847-1929) was another committed Christian. He said on one occasion, "If I had a hundred lives, they should be at Christ's disposal." Bobby Richardson, former baseball star for the New York Yankees, was also a man of commitment. He once prayed this prayer: "Dear Lord, Thy will, nothing more, nothing less, nothing else. Amen." All of these testimonies came from men who loved the Lord with all their minds, hearts, souls, and strength.

How much have you loved?—A reporter once asked Mother Teresa how she measured the success and failure of her work. She replied, "I don't think God uses categories like success and failure. His measurement is simply this: 'How much have you loved?' " That is the essence of what Jesus said in response to the question about the greatest commandment.

The impact of Christ.—Count Nikolaus Zinzendorf (b. 1700), born into Austrian nobility and trained for a career in the Saxony civil service, retired at the age of twenty-seven to his estate at Herrnhut and devoted himself to the Christian community he had started five years earlier for religious fugitives from Moravia. The spiritual fervor of his life was born out of a crisis when he was nineteen. He had just graduated in law, and he was sent off to complete his education by touring European cities. In Dusseldorf, he visited an art gallery, and he was captured by a masterly painting of Jesus. The eyes of Jesus seemed to penetrate Count Zinzendorf's heart. He was especially touched by the words written beneath the painting: "This I did for you; what are you doing for me?" Count Zinzendorf made a decision there and then to give his life in service for Christ. In every generation, from the first century to the present century, people of all levels of society and all kinds of backgrounds have been transformed by Christ and called into service for God.[2]

TEACHING THE CLASS

Main Idea: Love is the whole of the requirements of God.
Suggested Teaching Aim: Learners will examine their attitudes and commitment to love.

Introduce the Bible Study

Share the comments titled "How much have you loved?" (*Applying the Lesson*). Share information from the introduction to *Studying the Bible*. Write the main idea on the chalkboard.

State that the study for today uses terms with which most church members are familiar. Most know the teaching contained in the main idea. However, few are totally guided by love in living as followers of Christ. State that the purpose of the study is to help us examine our attitudes and our personal commitment to love. Invite learners to open their Bibles to Mark 12.

Search for Biblical Truth

Distribute copies of the following attitude survey and direct learners to mark their responses. If copies cannot be provided for each learner, read the statements aloud and ask each learner to write down a response.

1. Love is a feeling that you have toward God.
    Agree   Disagree
2. Love for other people is a feeling for them that is similar to the feeling you have toward God.
    Agree   Disagree
3. Love is something you do, not something you feel.
    Agree   Disagree
4. Love for God is obeying His commandments and teachings.
    Agree   Disagree
5. Love for others is doing what they want you to do.
    Agree   Disagree

State that while most people know that a requirement of God is that we love, there is much disagreement on exactly what that means. Note that the attitude survey is meant to point out such disagreement.

> **A Teaching Outline**
> 1. Focus on the Christian requirement to love.
> 2. Discover Jesus' explanation of the essential requirements of God.
> 3. Determine what a life of love looks like today.
> 4. Measure personal attitudes and commitment to determine if love is the whole of them.

Invite a learner to read Mark 12:28 aloud. Use information from *Studying the Bible* to set the scene indicated by this verse. Ask: What was the question from the scribe? See verse 28.

Call on a learner to read Jesus' response to the question in verses 30-31. Note the relationship of Jesus' words to the main idea written earlier on the chalkboard.

Call on a learner to read aloud the response of the scribe when he heard Jesus' words in verses 32-33. Ask: Does it seem strange that a scribe should think in this way? Why?

Note how Jesus responded to the scribe in verse 34. Ask: What do you think Jesus meant when He said the scribe was not far from the kingdom of God? (Consider this explanation: The scribe was open to truth.)

Note that the critics were now silenced and Jesus took the occasion to challenge them further. Call on a learner to read verses 35-37 aloud. Use information from *Studying the Bible* to explain His comments.

Give the Truth a Personal Focus

Share the comments titled "With the eyes open" (*Applying the Lesson*). Note that believers are more valuable with their eyes open to the truth about their attitudes and commitment to love. Ask: What does a life of love for God and others look like? Allow learners to ponder the question momentarily. Share comments from "True commitment" in *Applying the Lesson*.

Ask again: What does a life of love for God and others look like? Elicit response from learners.

Ask rhetorically: How does your day-to-day life measure up against that description? After a few moments for self-evaluation, share the comments titled "The impact of Christ" from *Applying the Lesson*.

---

1. Donald F. Ackland, *Studies in Deuteronomy* (Nashville, Convention Press, 1964), 54.
2. John R. W. Stott, *Focus on Christ* (Cleveland: William Collins Publishers, 1979), 136-38.

April 12

The Crucified Son of God

Basic Passage: Mark 15:1-41

Focal Passage: Mark 15:22-39

Suffering and death are not popular subjects. The majority of people try to banish them from their minds. As Christians, we have elected to make a cross the symbol of our faith, but for non-Catholics it is an empty cross, for we prefer to think about Easter morning rather than what happened at noonday three days before. Yet we dare not ignore the harsh realities of Good Friday, for the events of that day are at the very heart of gospel truth. Israel of old tried to explain away a portrait of the Messiah as "despised and rejected of men; a man of sorrows, and acquainted with grief" (Isa. 53:3). New Testament disciples closed their minds against their Master's own prediction of His approaching death in Jerusalem. However, the story of the crucified and risen Savior was to prove the message that would change human hearts and transform the world. Christ's disciples everywhere proclaimed that "God commendeth his love toward us, in that, while we were yet sinners, Christ died for us" (Rom. 5:8).

Study Aim: *To think about the price Jesus paid for our redemption and respond with faith, gratitude, and love*

STUDYING THE BIBLE

In order to match this lesson with the calendar, Good Friday and Easter being immediately ahead, we leap over several chapters of Mark's Gospel, all concerned with our Lord's activities in and around Jerusalem. Chapter 14 begins with mention of the approaching Feast of Passover and the grim information attached that "the chief priests and the scribes sought how they might take him by craft, and put him to death" (v. 1). They found a ready tool in one of the disciples, Judas, who plotted with them to betray his Master (vv. 10-11). In the garden of Gethsemane, their scheme was put into action by the identification and arrest of Jesus (vv. 32-52). This passage contains reference to "a certain young man" (vv. 51-52) whom some relate to Mark himself.

I. Jesus on Trial

Events moved swiftly, for our Lord's enemies were determined to complete their plan before news of what was happening reached the people. There were two trials, one ecclesiastical and the other civic, each of which can be broken down into three stages. It would be necessary to make a comparative study of all the Gospels to get the complete story.

1. **Before the Sanhedrin (14:53-65; 15:1).**—John's Gospel tells of a preliminary hearing before Annas, a former high priest (18:13). This was followed by an appearance before "the chief priests and all the council," that is, the Sanhedrin, the high court of the Jews (Mark 14:55). This body reached its predetermined verdict, declaring Jesus to be "guilty of death" (v. 64). Because its proceedings had been irregular, the law forbidding night meetings of the Sanhedrin, a hurried session was held the next morning (15:1) to confirm the action of the night.

2. **Before Pilate (15:2-15).**—The question addressed by the high priest to Jesus was, "Art thou the Christ, the Son of the Blessed?" (14:61). Pilate, the Roman governor, asked, "Art thou the King of the Jews?" (15:2). The charges brought before the two tribunals differed: the first was religious, the second, political. To gain Pilate's support for their murderous scheme, the Jewish leaders had presented Jesus as an insurrectionist, a threat to the authority of Rome. They took advantage of the moral weakness of Pilate who, though clearly wishing to release Jesus, yielded to their demands.

II. The Place of Execution (Mark 15:22-28)

Most sacred art shows our Lord carrying a complete cross along the road to Calvary. But it is now largely agreed that those condemned to death by crucifixion carried only the cross beam, the upright being already in place. The weight of this beam, however, was too much for Jesus who had been physically weakened by mistreatment. Mark added to information given by Matthew and Luke that "Simon a Cyrenian," who was enlisted to carry the cross beam, was "father of Alexander and Rufus" (v. 21), men who were apparently well known to Mark's readers. Paul, writing to the Christians of Rome, sent greetings to "Rufus chosen in the Lord" (Rom. 16:13), possibly one of these two sons.

> 22 And they bring him unto the place Golgotha, which is, being interpreted, The place of a skull.
> 23 And they gave him to drink wine mingled with myrrh: but he received it not.

24 And when they had crucified him, they parted his garments, casting lots upon them, what every man should take.
25 And it was the third hour, and they crucified him.
26 And the superscription of his accusation was written over, THE KING OF THE JEWS.
27 And with him they crucify two thieves; the one on his right hand, and the other on his left.
28 And the scripture was fulfilled, which saith, And he was numbered with the transgressors.

1. **Conscious humiliation (vv. 22-25).**—Two offers of drink are mentioned in our verses, and their difference needs to be recognized. In verse 23 Jesus was offered "wine mingled with myrrh," intended to relieve pain, and often provided by compassionate women to persons about to be crucified. This our Lord refused, choosing rather to be in full command of His senses. The other reference is to "a sponge full of vinegar" (v. 36), a cheap wine to assuage thirst. In full awareness therefore of the cruel proceedings, Jesus endured crucifixion, the agonizing details of which are played down by the inspired writer. The only reference is to the humiliation of being stripped as His garments were divided by the casting of lots among the executing squad of Roman soldiers. Mark recorded the time of day, 9:00 a.m.

2. **King on a cross (vv. 26-28).**—As verse 2 indicates, the charge made to Pilate against Jesus was that He had claimed kingship. It was customary for the charge to be displayed on the cross, largely as a warning to others against committing the same offense. But we may assume that Pilate took pleasure in the wording, "The King of the Jews," because of the embarrassment it would cause to our Lord's accusers. Only brief mention is made of the two men crucified with Jesus, here described as thieves. For a more detailed account, see Luke 23:39-43 where the two men are termed "malefactors," or evil doers. They may have engaged in violent revolt against Rome.

III. Mockery and Darkness (Mark 15:29-33)

This tragic scene is stated to have taken place at Golgotha, interpreted as "The place of a skull" (v. 22). This could have been a rocky prominence that had semblance to a skull. The word is Aramaic, and the Latin counterpart is Calvary. Its exact location is not known, although several sites have been suggested. Evidently it was near a highway as indicated by verse 29.

29 And they that passed by railed on him, wagging their heads, and saying, Ah, thou that destroyest the temple, and buildest it in three days,
30 Save thyself, and come down from the cross.

31 Likewise also the chief priests mocking said among themselves with the scribes, He saved others; himself he cannot save.

32 Let Christ the King of Israel descend now from the cross, that we may see and believe. And they that were crucified with him reviled him.

33 And when the sixth hour was come, there was darkness over the whole land until the ninth hour.

1. Unintended truth (vv. 29-32).—One of the accusations made against Jesus in the Sanhedrin trial was that He had said, "I am able to destroy the temple of God, and to build it in three days" (Matt. 26:61). An explanation of this is furnished in John 2:18-21, with its concluding words, "But he spake of the temple of his body." By perverse distortion of His meaning, His enemies turned this prophecy of His death and resurrection into an attack on the temple, the centuries-long shrine of the Jewish people, and a symbol of their national survival. By "He saved others" (v. 31), the chief priests and scribes referred to our Lord's miracles of healing, even raising the dead. But we are justified in seeing here a reference to spiritual salvation, which Jesus purchased for all who believe by the sacrifice of His life. He had to die that we might live.

2. The sixth hour (v. 33).—This would be noon when a three-hour period of darkness began. What forces of nature God employed to cast this dense shadow over the scene of His Son's death, we do not know. It lasted until Jesus surrendered Himself to death, a fitting response of creation to the darkest deed in history.

IV. A Roman's Testimony (Mark 15:34-39)

The solemn depths of our Lord's cry, "My God, my God, why hast thou forsaken me?" (v. 34) are difficult for us to plumb. In the physical darkness that enveloped Him, our Lord was plunged into a deeper spiritual darkness in which He realized momentarily the awful consequences of bearing humanity's load of sin. This was the price He paid as the world's Redeemer.

34 And at the ninth hour Jesus cried with a loud voice, saying, Eloi, Eloi, lama sabachthani? which is, being interpreted, My God, my God, why hast thou forsaken me?

35 And some of them that stood by, when they heard it, said, Behold, he calleth Elijah.

36 And one ran and filled a sponge full of vinegar, and put it on a reed, and gave him to drink, saying, Let alone; let us see whether Elijah will come to take him down.

37 And Jesus cried with a loud voice, and gave up the ghost.

38 And the veil of the temple was rent in twain from the top to the bottom.
39 And when the centurion, which stood over against him, saw that he so cried out, and gave up the ghost, he said, Truly this man was the Son of God.

Jesus spoke in Aramaic, which presumably accounted for the misunderstanding of those who thought He addressed Elijah. The rent veil is usually understood in light of Hebrews 9:2-12 and 10:19-20 as symbolic of the opening up of a way to God through Christ. Some see it, however, as a forecast of the coming destruction of the temple. The centurion's affirmation was desired by Mark from all who read his Gospel.

APPLYING THE LESSON

Death doesn't take a holiday.—A movie of 1930 vintage was called *Death Takes a Holiday.* In the movie, the angel of death spent a weekend on earth to see what it's like to be human. During this brief visit by the angel of death, the world was thrown into a panic. Without his help, people suffering from lingering illnesses couldn't die. The old and tired, who were begging for rest, could find no relief. Eventually, the angel of death went back to work, and the world returned to normal. The truth is: death does not take a holiday, not even when the Son of God lived on the earth. Jesus, too, faced the reality of death.

Turned the headlights on.—In a newspaper several years ago, this poignant letter from a family appeared on the obituary page: "Billy, you know it was just a year ago today that you left us, and the sunshine went out of our lives. But we turned on the headlights and are going on, and, Billy, we shall keep on doing the best we can until that glorious day when we'll see you again."[1]

That is the testimony of faith every Christian can voice. Why? Because when Jesus went into death, He did not stay there. When He faced death, He defeated death. Because He lives, we can live also.

Quick thinking.—The professor was aggravated at the young man who continually glanced at his watch during the professor's lecture. Deciding to embarrass the young man, he stopped his lecture and said, "Johnny, can you tell me why you look at your watch so often?" "Yes," Johnny replied, "because I was afraid you wouldn't have time to finish your interesting lecture!" He had to think quick to cover up his indiscretion.

The religious leaders who arrested Jesus in the night and brought Him to trial also had to do some quick thinking. Their actions were illegal, so they had to take additional steps to cover up their indiscretions.

Not when but what.—Someone has suggested that when suffering comes, the key question to ask is not When? but What? Instead of asking, "When am I going to get out of this?" we need to ask the question, "What am I going to get out of this?" Jesus' suffering on the cross went on for hours. However, the motivation that kept Him there was not the assumption it would soon be over but that through His sacrificial death on the cross He purchased eternal life for humankind.

Unable to write about the cross.—John Milton tried to write a poem on the cross but was unable to do so. He testified, "I will try no more. It is a never-ebbing sea in which our thoughts are drowned."[2] Henry Ward Beecher preached sermons on every aspect of Christ's life and many on the cross. But in no sermon did he describe the crucifixion. His biographer suggested that the cross was so sacred to Beecher that he never ventured to attempt a portrayal of it.[3]

Even though we cannot describe the cross, we must nevertheless declare the cross, for it is the heart of our gospel. Paul's beautiful statement to the Corinthians describes the impact of the cross: "He made Him who knew no sin to be sin on our behalf, that we might become the righteousness of God in Him" (2 Cor. 5:21, NASB).

How do you respond?—The cross demands a response in our lives. We see that response in the centurion who concluded Jesus was "the Son of God." We have seen that response in various other forms through the ages. A beautiful example is a simple man in a country church.

Many decades ago, a well-known preacher led a service in a country church one Sunday. He returned to his home on Monday. The next Saturday a man whom the preacher did not know knocked on his door. The man identified himself as the cook at the home where the preacher had eaten Sunday dinner. He said, "I heard you pray last Sunday noon that God would bless the hands that prepared the food. I looked down at these old hands, and tears came to my eyes. I decided to dedicate my hands to the Lord. All week long I have been working for the Lord, and I've never had so much fun in all my life. Now, I want you to pray that I may dedicate, not just my hands, but my whole life to Jesus."

TEACHING THE CLASS

Main Idea: Jesus' death requires a response of faith, gratitude, and love.

Suggested Teaching Aim: Learners will consider anew Jesus' death for them and respond with faith, gratitude, and love.

Introduce the Bible Study

Share the comments titled "Death doesn't take a holiday" from *Applying the Lesson*. Share information from the introduction to *Studying the Bible*.

If appropriate in your class, provide paper and markers for learners. Direct them to draw a representation of death. Give no further directions. Allow several minutes for learners to complete the assignment with some thought. When finished, invite them to share the pictures

APRIL 12, 1992

and their thoughts with those sitting near them. Invite some learners to share their drawing with the group.

> **A Teaching Outline**
> 1. Raise the issue of death.
> 2. Examine the circumstances and incidents surrounding the death of Jesus.
> 3. Determine the response demanded by the death of Jesus.
> 4. Respond to Jesus with renewed faith, gratitude, and love.

Note that the study for today relates to the death of Jesus. Ask: Do you think that Jesus felt differently about death than you do? Did He dread it any less? Wait for response. State that the purpose of the study is to remind us of the price that Jesus paid when He died for us and to help us consider again how we should respond to what He did for us.

Search for Biblical Truth

Invite learners to open their Bibles to Mark 14. Note that many events precede the passage to be studied today. Call attention to the following outline that has been displayed.

The Crucified Son of God
I. Jesus on trial
   A. Before the Sanhedrin (Mark 14:53-65; 15:1)
   B. Before Pilate (Mark 15:2-15)
II. The execution
   A. Conscious humiliation (Mark 15:22-25)
   B. King on a cross (Mark 15:26-28)
III. Mockery and Darkness
   A. Mocking words; unintended truth (Mark 15:29-32)
   B. Deathly darkness (Mark 15:33)
IV. Death
   A. A cry of anguish (Mark 15:34-36)
   B. Death prevails (Mark 15:37-38)
   C. A Roman soldier's testimony (Mark 15:39)

Use the outline to examine the circumstances and incidents surrounding the death of Jesus. When the trials of Jesus are reviewed, use the comments titled "Quick thinking" (*Applying the Lesson*). When Jesus' suffering on the cross is reviewed, use the comments titled "Not when but what" (*Applying the Lesson*).

Give the Truth a Personal Focus

Share the comments titled "Unable to write about the cross" (*Applying the Lesson*). Ask: What response does the death of Jesus on the cross demand from you and me? Ask for response. Faith, gratitude, and love should be included. Use the comments titled "How do you respond?" (*Applying the Lesson*). Ask rhetorically: Have you responded to the death of Jesus for you with your whole life? yes

---

1. Paul Powell, *Why Me, Lord?* (Wheaton, Ill.: Victor Books, 1981), 72.
2. James Wesberry, *Evangelistic Sermons* (Nashville: Broadman Press, 1973), 12.
3. Lyman Abbott, *Henry Ward Beecher* (Cambridge: The Riverside Press, 1903), 117.

April 19

An Empty Tomb

Basic Passage: Mark 15:42—16:8

Focal Passage: Mark 15:42—16:8

This is our final lesson from Mark's Gospel. Its theme is triumphant, for it deals with our Lord's resurrection. Our major focus will be on that event with its message of life beyond death and victory in Christ over all that opposes God's eternal purposes. But another interesting matter is forced on our attention. Did Mark's Gospel end at 16:8 as many believe? This belief is expressed in the *New* International Version by the statement "The most reliable early manuscripts and other ancient witnesses do not have Mark 16:9-20." The problem is briefly discussed later in these comments, so it will suffice to say here that probably the concluding section of the Gospel was somehow lost. Fortunately, we have three other Gospels to inform us of happenings after the resurrection. The likely loss of a few verses at the end of one Gospel serves to emphasize the marvel of the preservation of the Word of God through the centuries. The discovery of the Dead Sea Scrolls, in 1947, furnished new evidence of divine protection of the sacred books so that we may read them today with confidence in their authenticity.

Study Aim: *To share with all Christians the joy of Easter and the hope of life everlasting*

STUDYING THE BIBLE

In a brief summary of the gospel he preached, the apostle Paul wrote of our Lord, "Christ died for our sins . . . was buried, and . . . rose again the third day" (1 Cor. 15:3-4). The statement "was buried" may appear superfluous. However, Paul had heard the claims of some opponents of the gospel that Jesus did not really die, but only swooned. The three-day interment of the body corrected this falsehood. So, likewise, the Gospel writers provided details of the proceedings that led to the depositing of Jesus' lifeless body in Joseph's tomb.

I. A Tomb Provided (Mark 15:42-46)

Normally, the Romans left the bodies of the crucified to decompose, or be eaten as carrion, and to furnish shocking warnings of the kind of justice meted out to the condemned. On occasion they turned the remains over to friends or relatives for decent burial. Jewish law forbade bodies of hanged persons being left overnight (Deut. 21:22-23). In our Lord's case, the beginning of the Sabbath (6:00 p.m.) being near, there was reason for swift action.

> 42 And now when the even was come, because it was the preparation, that is, the day before the sabbath,
> 43 Joseph of Arimathaea, an honorable counselor, which also waited for the kingdom of God, came, and went in boldly unto Pilate, and craved the body of Jesus.
> 44 And Pilate marveled if he were already dead: and calling unto him the centurion, he asked him whether he had been any while dead.
> 45 And when he knew it of the centurion, he gave the body to Joseph.
> 46 And he bought fine linen, and took him down, and wrapped him in the linen, and laid him in a sepulcher which was hewn out of a rock, and rolled a stone unto the door of the sepulcher.

1. Joseph's request (vv. 42-43).—As a respected member of the Sanhedrin, Joseph would have some standing with Pilate. He was among those who, like Simeon (Luke 2:25), lived in expectation of the coming of Messiah. Joseph is not claimed as a disciple; yet by his action, he made strong public commitment to Jesus.

2. **Pilate's surprise (vv. 44-45).**—Death was normally slow for victims of crucifixion, which added to the cruelty of this form of punishment. Although death was largely the result of exhaustion, verse 37 describes Jesus as crying "with a loud voice" (see John 19:30); at this point He surrendered His life in the knowledge that His redemptive work was accomplished.

3. **Burial care (v. 46).**—Joseph's action was premeditated, for he had bought "fine linen" in which to wrap our Lord's body. The tomb was probably intended for his own use and was in the nature of a small room hewn out of natural rock. To discourage grave robbers, a heavy stone could be rolled over the opening. This fulfilled Isaiah's prophecy, "he made his grave . . . with the rich in his death" (Isa. 53:9).

II. Women at the Tomb (Mark 15:47; 16:1)

Significant tribute is paid by Mark to the loyalty of several women to the crucified Jesus (15:40-41). He does not mention Mary, our Lord's mother, who was present at Calvary and was given, by Jesus, into the care of the apostle John (John 19:25-27). But he named three who observed His burial and came later to the tomb to render normal services to the dead.

> 47 And Mary Magdalene and Mary the mother of Joses beheld where he was laid.
> 1 And when the sabbath was past, Mary Magdalene, and Mary the mother of James, and Salome, had bought sweet spices, that they might come and anoint him.

1. **Love standing watch (15:47).**—Mary Magdalene, or Mary from Magdala, is later described as she from "whom he had cast seven devils" (16:9; Luke 8:2). Mary the mother of James should probably be identified with "the wife of Cleophas" (John 19:25). Salome is generally regarded as the mother of James and John, wife of Zebedee, and perhaps sister to Mary, our Lord's mother. We know nothing about the "many other women" (15:41) but salute them as faithful friends who ministered to our Lord's needs both before and after His death.

2. **Ministry to the dead (16:1).**—Embalming was not practiced among the Jews, but it was customary to anoint corpses with perfumed oils. Although John 19:38-40 describes Joseph and Nicodemus (unmentioned by Mark) as rendering this service, the women were not satisfied until they had added their own tribute of love, which they set out to do early in the day following the Sabbath. As events happened, their anointing was no longer needed.

III. Easter Morning at the Tomb (Mark 16:2-7)

Although the Gospel records differ in detail as to what happened at that early hour, all agree that something tremendous had occurred between the entombment on Friday evening and the women's visit the morning after the Sabbath. For when the women arrived, the tomb was empty, and the news awaiting them was that Christ had risen.

> 2 And very early in the morning the first day of the week, they came unto the sepulcher at the rising of the sun.
> 3 And they said among themselves, Who shall roll away the stone from the door of the sepulcher?
> 4 And when they looked, they saw that the stone was rolled away: for it was very great.
> 5 And entering into the sepulcher, they saw a young man sitting on the right side, clothed in a long white garment; and they were affrighted.
> 6 And he saith unto them, Be not affrighted: Ye seek Jesus of Nazareth, which was crucified: he is risen; he is not here: behold the place where they laid him.
> 7 But go your way, tell his disciples and Peter that he goeth before you into Galilee: there shall ye see him, as he said unto you.

1. Facing difficulty (vv. 2-4).—The problem of the heavy stone that covered the entrance to the tomb did not deter the women from their mission of love. Mark, who recorded what happened, probably heard the story again and again from the women assembled with other Christians in his mother's home (Acts 12:12); "for it was very great" sounds like a personal memory.

2. Heavenly messenger (vv. 5-6).—Who other than an angel from God could be the qualified announcer of our Lord's resurrection? He invited the women to view the empty tomb and the very place where earlier (15:47) they had seen His body laid. Also the angel told of the fulfillment of our Lord's promise (14:28) that He would meet them in Galilee. We learn from other writers that there were postresurrection visits with the disciples before the Galilee rendezvous.

3. Special to Peter (v. 7).—In view of Peter's denials (14:66-72), the personal message to this disciple was specially gracious. It brought assurance that all was not over between him and his Lord, but the future held promise of resumed fellowship and forgiveness.

IV. An Abrupt Conclusion (Mark 16:8)

Were the words, "for they were afraid," Mark's intended ending for his Gospel, or did he write more? Has his conclusion to chapter 16 been lost? Scholars are generally agreed that verses 9-20 are not original to this Gospel but a later addition, written by someone who based what he wrote on the conclusions to the other Gospels. Users of the *New Revised Standard Version* will find printed not only this longer conclusion but also a shorter one that is found in some ancient manuscripts.

> **8 And they went out quickly, and fled from the sepulcher; for they trembled and were amazed: neither said they anything to any man; for they were afraid.**

Can we accept this as an appropriate ending to Mark's Gospel? Many competent authorities feel that they can. Others think that for Mark to end on this negative note would be out of harmony with the purpose of the author to present our Lord as "The Strong Son of God" (this quarter's theme). Accordingly, and in line with the most reliable manuscripts which end with verse 8, the following two suggestions are offered: Mark wrote more, but his final verses were lost (perhaps through accidental damage to the manuscript, which would have been in the form of a scroll); Mark did not live to finish his Gospel, but he became a martyr under Nero. Unless some great archaeological discovery comes to our aid, we will probably never know the answer to this problem. But we may be grateful that the Markan record, whether complete or not, bears witness with the other Gospels, to the reality of Christ's resurrection, "He is risen" (v. 6).

APPLYING THE LESSON

The accuracy of God's Word.—In 1947, Bedouin herdsmen discovered a cave near the Dead Sea in Palestine that was filled with scrolls. These scrolls happened to be ancient manuscripts of the Bible. Portions of all the Old Testament books except Esther were found. In addition, these caves contained commentaries on the Old Testament books, writings that set forth the ethical teachings of the group who collected the manuscripts, and writings about their hopes for the future. These manuscripts, some more than one thousand years older than any previously known biblical manuscripts, have confirmed the accuracy and dependability of the translations of the Bible we Christians use today.

An incredible opinion.—Some skeptics of the resurrection have suggested another explanation of what happened that first Easter Sunday morning, an explanation that is more incredible than the biblical message. According to this "swoon theory," Jesus did not really die but instead merely swooned on the cross. He was revived by the cool atmosphere of the tomb and the odor of the spices. Consequently, he escaped from the tomb and convinced the disciples He was alive. How incredible to believe that after Jesus had been beaten and humiliated all night, after He had been flogged, and after He had spent several hours nailed to the cross, He could still have enough physical strength to untie himself from the grave clothes that bound Him hand and foot, somehow push away the stone from the inside of the tomb, overcome the Roman guards stationed to watch the tomb, and then appear to the disciples in such a powerful way that He could convince them He had been raised up from the dead! Some people will believe anything!

We're not about success.—Clarence Jordan was a Christian with both unusual abilities and unique commitment. He had two Ph.D.'s, one in agriculture and one in biblical languages. A world of opportunities was out before him. He chose to give his life in service to the poor. He moved to Americus, Georgia, back in the 1940s, and founded a farm where poor whites and blacks could work together to provide for the needs of their families. He called it Koinonia Farm. Jordan's effort was resisted by the local citizens. They boycotted him, slashed the workers' tires when they came to town, and tried everything they could to sabotage the work. For fourteen years, Jordan continued his ministry to the poor. Finally, in 1954, the Ku Klux Klan decided to get rid of him once and for all. They came at night with guns and torches and burned every building on Koinonia Farm except Clarence Jordan's home, which they riddled with bullets. The next day, a local newspaper reporter came to see what remained of the farm. Clarence Jordan recognized the reporter's voice as one of the men who had attacked his farm the night before. Clarence Jordan was in the field, hoeing and planting. Surprised that Clarence was still around, the reporter said, "Well, Dr. Jordan, you got two of them Ph.D.'s, you've put fourteen years into this farm, and there's nothing left of it at all. Just how successful do you think you've been?" Clarence stopped hoeing, turned to the reporter, and answered, "Sir, I don't think you understand us. What we are about is not success but faithfulness."[1]

When Jesus went to the cross, some of the women were standing by. Their hopes had been dashed and their dreams shattered. Yet they remained faithful.

The use of spices.—Two spices specifically mentioned in the New Testament in anointing a body for burial are myrrh and aloes. Myrrh was a fragrant substance derived from a certain balsam tree. Apparently it was available in liquid and solid forms. Aloes was an aromatic substance derived from a sandalwood tree. It was used for perfume and for anointing bodies at death. Other spices that may have been used for anointing a body at burial were balm, gum, and nard. Ointments also were used to prepare a body for burial. In Israel, olive oil was the main ingredient in ointments. To the olive oil, various perfumes were added. The raw material then was crushed, boiled, and stirred. Ointments were smeared on the body. Spices were wrapped in a linen shroud used to cover the body. Such were the spices the women took to the tomb to anoint the body of Jesus.

TEACHING THE CLASS

Main Idea: Jesus died on the cross, was buried, and resurrected after three days.

Suggested Teaching Aim: Learners will explain the work of redemption carried out in the death and resurrection of Jesus.

Introduce the Bible Study

Write these words on the chalkboard: *Resurrection, Redemption, Salvation, Eternal Life.* Ask: What do these words have to do with Easter? Wait for their response.

Continue by asking: Do most people have accurate understanding of the meaning of these words? Do you? If you were required to explain the work of redemption through the death and resurrection of Jesus to someone who did not understand "churchy" words, could you do so?

A Teaching Outline
1. Focus on redemption and its meaning.
2. Identify the events of resurrection morning and their meaning for redemption.
3. Explain the redemptive nature of the events of Jesus' death and resurrection.
4. Recommit to faithfulness as a response of gratitude.

State that as we study the wonderful happenings of the first Easter morning, our purpose is to increase our ability to explain the work of redemption carried out in the death and resurrection of Jesus. Invite learners to open their Bibles to Mark 15.

Search for Biblical Truth

Share the comments titled "The accuracy of God's Word" (*Applying the Lesson*). Note that today's study picks up where it ended last Sunday. Review the outline displayed to guide the Scripture study last Sunday. Display this outline of the events that followed.

A Glorious, Empty Tomb
I. A tomb provided
  A. Joseph's request (Mark 15:42-43)
  B. Pilate's surprise (Mark 15:44-45)
  C. Burial care (Mark 15:46)
II. Women at the tomb
  A. Love standing watch (Mark 15:47)
  B. Ministry to the dead (Mark 16:1)
III. Easter morning at the tomb
  A. An early morning visit (Mark 16:2-4)
  B. A heavenly messenger (Mark 16:5-6)
  C. A special message to Peter (Mark 16:7)
  D. An abrupt conclusion (Mark 16:8)

Use the outline to study the Scripture that tells of Jesus' burial and resurrection. When the request to bury Jesus is discussed, use the comments titled "An incredible option" (*Applying the Lesson*). When the trip of the women to the tomb is discussed, note their faithfulness even when their hopes had been dashed. Share the comments titled "We're not about success" (*Applying the Lesson*). Also share information titled "The use of spices" (Applying the Lesson) to explain the mission of the women that Easter morning.

Give the Truth a Personal Focus

Remind the learners of the words written on the chalkboard as the study was begun. Assign each word to a small group of learners for a word study. Direct them to use the resources in their own Bibles, such as a concordance or dictionary. Provide additional resources for use during this time from your church media center. Direct the learners to write an explanation of the word assigned to them that does not use "churchy" language. When the word study is finished, invite groups to share what they have written.

Ask: If you used these kinds of explanations, would you be able to explain the redemptive nature of the death and resurrection of Jesus more clearly? Call on two learners who will role play a conversation in which one explains to the other what Jesus' death and resurrection means and invites him or her to personally accept the salvation that this provides. It may be helpful to arrange before the class meeting for two learners to do this role play.

Recall the faithfulness of the women. Note that gratitude for what Jesus did for us demands faithfulness. Invite learners to recommit themselves to this miraculously risen Savior.

---

1. Tim Hansel, *Holy Sweat* (Waco: Word Books, 1987), 188-89.

March, April, May 1992

God's People in the World

Aids from BROADMAN for Studying and Teaching

Books:
A Guide for New Testament Study, William Stevens
The Broadman Bible Commentary, Volume 12
Layman's Bible Book Commentary, Volume 23

   The quarter will be brought to a close by studies in the Epistles of Peter, the first of which was addressed to a persecuted church. Our themes will vary from words of comfort and hope to exhortations to live worthily in an unfriendly world. A strong emphasis will appear on the doctrine of our Lord's return and what this means to the church and the world.

April 26

The Gift of Living Hope

Basic Passage: 1 Peter 1:1-25

Focal Passages: 1 Peter 1:3-9,13-21

After a series of lessons on the Gospel of Mark, much of whose material is believed to have been provided by Peter, it is appropriate that we conclude the quarter with studies in the writings of Peter himself. While we cannot ascribe exact dates for either writings, it seems likely that they were both authored around the same time, between A.D. 60 and 67. The two men addressed themselves to different audiences, for while Mark wrote to Christians in Rome, the apostle Peter named his readers as residents in the five Roman provinces listed in 1:1, spread out along the shores of Asia Minor and the Black Sea. Apparently, the Christians in these areas were enduring persecution, of what sort and from what source is not stated, whether general or local we cannot tell. The apostle responded to the need for encouragement and exhortation of believers under pressure, coupled with a call to consistent Christian living, whatever the circumstances. The two concluding verses of the epistle helpfully summarize its message.

Study Aim: *To learn how to stand strong in faith and loyalty in an unbelieving and unfriendly society*

STUDYING THE BIBLE

The First Epistle of Peter belongs to what is known as the "persecution literature" of the New Testament. We need to be reminded of the price early believers paid for their faithfulness, that Christians in some parts of the world are paying that price today, and that prevailing indifference in our culture could easily change to open hostility in the near future.

I. A Christian's Privileges (1 Pet. 1:1-12)

The opening verse is clear with one exception: Who are "the strangers"? The NRSV reads, "exiles of the Dispersion." "Dispersion" (*diaspora*) is usually employed to describe Jews living outside the Holy Land. There are also indications that Peter wrote to others besides Jews. Verses 14 and 18 are more readily applied to Gentiles converted from paganism than to Jews. It is possible to conclude, therefore, that Peter wrote for both Jewish and Gentiles readers and that the "Dispersion" he referred to was that of all believers who, while in this life, are exiles from their future heavenly home. He thought of them all in the exalted terms of verse 2.

> 3 Blessed be the God and Father of our Lord Jesus Christ, which according to his abundant mercy hath begotten us again unto a lively hope by the resurrection of Jesus Christ from the dead,
> 4 To an inheritance incorruptible, and undefiled, and that fadeth not away, reserved in heaven for you,
> 5 Who are kept by the power of God through faith unto salvation ready to be revealed in the last time.
> 6 Wherein ye greatly rejoice, though now for a season, if need be, ye are in heaviness through manifold temptations:
> 7 That the trial of your faith, being much more precious than of gold that perisheth, though it be tried with fire, might be found unto praise and honor and glory at the appearing of Jesus Christ:
> 8 Whom having not seen, ye love; in whom, though now ye see him not, yet believing, ye rejoice with joy unspeakable and full of glory:
> 9 Receiving the end of your faith, even the salvation of your souls.

1. Prospect (vv. 3-4).—Following an outburst of praise to "the God and Father of our Lord Jesus Christ," Peter wrote of the "living hope" (NRSV) of believers, the result of their having been "begotten . . . again," that is, born again. This living hope is grounded in the resurrection of our Lord, in whose rising again we have hope for life everlasting. The believer's hope will have fulfillment in heaven where he or she will enter into an inheritance that, unlike earthly bequests, will also have everlasting qualities.

2. Security (vv. 5-9).—The guarantee of this future blessing is found in "the power of God" so that those who exercise faith may be sure of attaining salvation in its fullest and ultimate sense. This will be in spite of "various trials" (v. 6, NRSV) that may cause great "heaviness," or distress, but these will come to be recognized as opportunities for demonstrating unwavering faith in God. When the Lord Jesus returns, this overcoming faith will be acknowledged with "praise and honor and glory."

3. Advantages (vv. 10-12).—The several references to salvation in these verses contemplate the completion of God's work of grace in and for the believer. We are saved when we believe in and receive the Lord Jesus as Savior. But the ultimate advantages of salvation will not be known until we enter into God's presence in our heavenly home. Then we shall experience that which even the prophets were unable to comprehend (v. 10) and angels long to understand (v. 12). Though wiser than us, angels know nothing of the joy of being redeemed by the sacrifice of God's Son.

II. A Christian's Responsibilities (1 Pet. 1:13-17)

God's work of grace in the believer, with its glorious prospect for the future, imposes certain obligations on those who are the beneficiaries. Life can no longer be lived as before, in the indulgence of "former lusts" (v. 14), but must be made to conform to the character of God Himself, whose nature is holy.

> 13 Wherefore gird up the loins of your mind, be sober, and hope to the end for the grace that is to be brought unto you at the revelation of Jesus Christ;
> 14 As obedient children, not fashioning yourselves according to the former lusts in your ignorance:
> 15 But as he which hath called you is holy, so be ye holy in all manner of conversation;
> 16 Because it is written, Be ye holy; for I am holy.
> 17 And if ye call on the Father, who without respect of persons judgeth according to every man's work, pass the time of your sojourning here in fear.

1. Alertness (v. 13a).—The exhortation to "gird up the loins of your mind" reflected the practice in those long-robed times of tucking the skirt of a garment into the waistband in readiness for work to be done. We might say, "Pull yourselves together," in a spiritual sense, for the exhortation is linked with "the revelation of Jesus Christ," that is, His coming again. Christians are always to be in a state of readiness for the Lord's return.

2. Self-control (v. 13b).—To "be sober" suggests avoidance of intoxication, which the apostle may well have intended. But we should probably understand a wider meaning, that is, a call to self-disciplined living. If this call was necessary in those days, when believers lived in a pagan society, surely it is no less necessary today.

3. Expectancy (v. 13c).—Christian hope is to be focused on the promised return of Christ. New Testament writers constantly urged this upon their readers, and although nearly two thousand years have passed since then, the possibility of our Lord's sudden return should still influence our behavior. This was the next point made by Peter to his readers.

4. Holiness (vv. 14-17).—Obedience to Christ means the abandonment of former life-styles when these do not conform to His teaching and example; "conversation" means life-style. Holiness is being set apart from all that is evil, and it belongs to the character of God Himself. The thought of having to give account to Him (v. 17) should help us in practicing this separateness from the world and its ways.

III. A Christian's Indebtedness (1 Pet. 1:18-25)

Gratitude should inspire the believer to appropriate conduct for a follower of the crucified Son of God. Peter described Jesus' redemptive work as the payment of a ransom, money paid to secure the release of a captive. Only, in Christ's case, the payment was made, not in money, but in the surrender of His life by the shedding of His blood.

> 18 Forasmuch as ye know that ye were not redeemed with corruptible things, as silver and gold, from your vain conversation received by tradition from your fathers;
> 19 But with the precious blood of Christ, as of a lamb without blemish and without spot:
> 20 Who verily was foreordained before the foundation of the world, but was manifest in these last times for you,
> 21 Who by him do believe in God, that raised him up from the dead, and gave him glory; that your faith and hope might be in God.

1. Salvation's cost (vv. 18-19).—That Peter's readers were ransomed "from the futile ways inherited from your ancestors" (NRSV) could refer to either Jews or Gentiles. God saw value in them and paid the price of their deliverance from those futile ways by the offering of His Son. The Old Testament sacrificial system (v. 19) is in view as Jesus took the place ("once for all," Heb. 10:10) of the slain lamb whose death was accepted as atonement for sins committed.

2. Salvation's plan (vv. 20-21).—Quoting Ray Summers, "That which God had planned before the creation of the world, he brought to reality at a point in history through the death and resurrection of Jesus Christ."[1] It was *faith* in Jesus as Savior that had produced in Peter's readers the *hope* of life everlasting. Note that the salvation experience begins with God and ends with God, for it was the Father's purpose that sent the Son to live and die for our sakes.

3. Salvation's agent (vv. 22-25).—To the list of Christian responsibilities in verses 13-17, Peter added love for one another. He described this as "unfeigned love," which is genuine and not superficial. Such love results from having been "born again," and as in our Lord's discourse with Nicodemus (John 3), not in a human sense but as the result of insemination with a divine seed, none other than "the word of God." Peter had in mind the preaching of the gospel through which his readers had learned of Christ and put their faith in Him. For us there is the additional truth: through becoming acquainted with "the word of God" in written and printed form, people may receive eternal blessing.

APPLYING THE LESSON

Response to suffering.—One writer described five ways we attempt to escape the grasp of suffering. First, we plead. We ask God to be fair with us. What we are really asking is for God to deal kindly with us, regardless of how He deals with others. Second, we compare. We point out to God how much better we are than others with the implication being that God should therefore be treating us better than He is. Third, we pout. When steps one and two bring no relief, we often pout. We have a pity party and feel sorry for ourselves. Fourth, we shout. How often do we become angry at God and shake our fist in His face? Fifth, we doubt. When the other steps do not change our circumstances, we often become disenchanted with God. We begin to doubt if He is able to help us or if He cares enough about us to help us.[2]

How should we respond? Peter's message is that we should expect suffering, endure it through God's power, and emerge from it better equipped to serve Him.

God carries us through.—One of the most beautiful stories of God's provision is the story of a man who had a dream. In his dream, he pictured his whole life flashing across the sky. Below this panorama of the events of his life, he pictured God walking by his side along the beach, and as they walked along, they left footprints on the sand. But every time an experience of suffering flashed across the sky, the man noticed only one set of footprints on the sand. So he cried out to God, "Why is it that you leave me when suffering comes? Why is it that you leave me to walk alone during the tough times of my life?" God answered, "In those times when you see only one set of footprints on the sand, they are not your footprints. They are Mine. I do not leave you during those times. Those are the times when I carry you through." Peter's hope in this week's text is based on the confidence that God will carry us through the experiences of suffering in our lives.

The great teacher of life.—Life's greatest teacher is not pleasure but suffering. In our suffering, we learn lessons we could not learn otherwise. Let me give two expressions of that truth.

Helen Keller once said about her physical handicaps, "I thank God for my handicaps, for through them I have found myself, my work, and my God." The same truth is expressed in an oft-used poem:

> I walked a mile with Pleasure,
> She chattered all the way,
> But left me none the wiser
> For all she had to say.
>
> I walked a mile with Sorrow,
> And ne'er a word said she;
> But, oh, the things I learned from her
> When Sorrow walked with me![3]

Letting God have your life. George W. Truett was one of the greatest of Southern Baptist preachers, but his pilgrimage of faith began just like that of every other individual, with a willingness to give his heart to God. He explained his feelings the morning after his conversion experience. Before getting up from bed, he said these thoughts ran through his mind: "Last night you made a public profession of religion. Now, the neighborhood knows about it, or will know about it, ere the day is done. What have you to say about your public profession of Christ, as your Savior and Master, this morning?" He put himself to this test: "What if Christ should now visibly come into this room, and put to you this question, 'Are you willing for me to have my way with your life, from this time on? I will not indicate to you what that way is to be—it is enough for you to know that my way is always right and safe and best. May I have your consent, without evasion or reservation, to have my way with you now and always?' " Truett gave this answer, "To such tests, I gave my unreserved 'Yes,' and a great peace filled my heart."[4]

That kind of unreserved commitment to God is necessary for Him to do in us and through us what He wants to do.

TEACHING THE CLASS

Main Idea: Hope is based on new life in Christ.
Suggested Teaching Aim: Learners will, based on their life in Christ, renew their hope in the face of life concerns.

Introduce the Bible Study

Use information from *Studying the Bible* to introduce the new unit of study in 1 Peter. State that the quarter will be concluded with the unit titled "Confession and Crucifixion."

Write *Hope* on the chalkboard. Ask: In what ways is hope vital to the life of all men? Elicit response. Continue by asking: Why do Christians emphasize hope as a vital part of their faith? Wait for response.

State that the study for today focuses on the basis for hope in the believer's life. Invite learners to open their Bibles to 1 Peter 1.

Search for Biblical Truth

State that 1 Peter 1:3-9 reflects a strong basis for hope in the life of believers. Call on a learner to read verses 3-4 aloud. When the reading is finished, ask: What reason for hope among believers is suggested here? (everlasting life in heaven). Ask: Why can Christians be confident in this hope of heaven? (Note v. 3.)

> **A Teaching Outline**
> 1. Introduce the new unit of study.
> 2. Focus on the function of hope in believers' lives.
> 3. Discover the basis for hope when there is new life in Jesus.
> 4. Plan ways to renew personal hope in the midst of today's concerns.
> 5. Praise God for the reason for hope.

Note that a second reason for hope is given in verse 5. Call on a learner to read the verse aloud. Ask: Why can believers be confident in their hope of heaven? (They are kept by the power of God.) Share the comments titled "God carries us through" (*Applying the Lesson*).

Mention that the hope of believers is not developed through ease and comfort but through difficult times. Call on someone to read verses 6-9. Share the comments titled "Response to suffering" (*Applying the Lesson*).

Write *responsibility* on the chalkboard. State that the hope provided believers through confidence in Jesus Christ also carries responsibility. Write these words on the chalkboard beneath "responsibility": *alertness, self-control, expectancy,* and *holiness*. Direct learners to read verses 13-17 silently and match the words and the verses. After a few minutes of study, call for response.

Write *indebtedness* on the chalkboard. Call on a learner to read verses 18-25 aloud. Direct others to listen to discover what the indebtedness of believers is. When the reading is finished, call for response. After their response, share the comments titled "Letting God have your life" found in *Applying the Lesson*.

Give the Truth a Personal Focus

Share the comments titled "The great teacher of life" (*Applying the Lesson*). Note that in times of adversity and suffering, hope can become the most precious. Ask: Does your hope bloom or wither when you experience difficult times in your life? Why?

Suggest that learners talk with those sitting near them to determine ways to sustain and renew hope in the midst of personal stress and difficulties. After a few minutes of discussion, invite learners to share their conclusions. Include such things as remembering their security in Christ, recalling their home in heaven, and rejoicing in their present salvation. Conclude with a time of praise to God for the reasons learners have for their hope in Christ.

---

1. Ray Summers, "1 Peter" in *The Broadman Bible Commentary,* vol. 12 (Nashville: Broadman Press, 1972), 153.

2. Patrick M. Morley, *The Man in the Mirror* (Brentwood, Tenn.: Wolgemuth and Hyatt Publishers, 1989), 240-41.
3. Robert Browning Hamilton, "Pleasure and Sorrow," *Masterpieces of Religious Verse*, ed. James D. Morrison (Nashville: Broadman Press, 1977), 436
4. Powhatan James, *George W. Truett* (New York: The MacMillan Co., 1939), 25.

May 3

Called to Be God's People

Basic Passage: 1 Peter 2:1-25

Focal Passage: 1 Peter 2:1-10

Deep spiritual truths are mingled with practical advice on Christian living in this letter by Peter. Both are needed if we are to become mature in the faith. We need to realize that at the time Peter wrote his epistle the temple in Jerusalem was still standing. Its priestly officials, ornate furnishings, and impressive style of worship made the simple assemblies of Christians look inadequate, specially to Jewish converts. Gentile believers also were faced with a similar unfavorable comparison, for the pagan temples were staffed by elegant officials and their rituals outclassed the uncomplicated ordinances of New Testament churches. Peter wanted his readers to know there was no reason for any sense of inferiority. Christians were part of a massive change from the old to the new in which the church of Jesus Christ assumed roles that belonged to others in the past. The consequent spiritual privileges with which the individual believer was invested called for a life-style worthy of the faith professed.

Study Aim: *To better understand the God-given status of believers and respond with disciplined living*

STUDYING THE BIBLE

The high spiritual tone of this epistle is remarkable with Peter as its author, causing some to deny that he wrote it. But the rash, unpredictable disciple of the Gospels became a transformed man at Pentecost.

His consequent leadership position in the Jerusalem church testified to his emotional and spiritual development. Peter is, in fact, an outstanding example of his teaching that Christians should "grow in grace" (2 Pet. 3:18).

I. Growing in Grace (1 Pet. 2:1-3)

No break is intended between chapters 1 and 2. The chapter divisions, while convenient, sometimes interrupt the flow of what the writer is saying. This is largely overcome, in this case, by the opening word of chapter 2, whether we read it as "Wherefore" (KJV) or "Therefore" (NASB, NIV). Because you have been "born again" (1:23), Peter said, there are certain consequences for life and conduct.

> 1 Wherefore laying aside all malice, and all guile, and hypocrisies, and envies, and all evil speakings,
> 2 As newborn babes, desire the sincere milk of the word, that ye may grow thereby:
> 3 If so be ye have tasted that the Lord is gracious.

1. Hindrances to growth (v. 1).—All of these listed are sins of the disposition, the subtler sins that may characterize persons who would avoid physical violence and sins of the flesh. The list may read, "malice, . . . guile, . . . insincerity, . . . envy, and . . . slander" (NRSV). These are to be "put away" (RSV), indicating an act of the will, in which, of course, we need to ask God's help. The popular slogan, "Say no," applies here.

2. Means of growth (vv. 2-3).—The remedy for wrong behavior is the right nourishment, what Peter called "the pure, spiritual milk" (NRSV). That he spoke of his readers as "newborn babes" would suggest that these were new converts who so far had only "tasted that the Lord is gracious." What they had experienced, however, should give them an appetite for more. As milk nourishes a young child, and produces growth, so the Word of God feeds the believer who thereby develops into maturity.

II. Endowed with Dignity (1 Pet. 2:4-10)

In 4:14, Peter wrote of his readers that they were "reproached for the name of Christ." In their daily lives they were subjected to indignities, so the apostle reminded them of their high standing before God. His repeated use of Old Testament concepts affirmed the truth that these Christians, whether Jews or Gentiles, were God's chosen people, the new Israel. Metaphors are mixed in this passage, which begins with a call to come to Christ, in faith and fellowship, that in Him they might be built up into a spiritual house.

4 To whom coming, as unto a living stone, disallowed indeed of men, but chosen of God, and precious;

5 Ye also, as lively stones, are built up a spiritual house, an holy priesthood, to offer up spiritual sacrifices, acceptable to God by Jesus Christ.

6 Wherefore also it is contained in the scripture, Behold, I lay in Zion a chief corner stone, elect, precious: and he that believeth on him shall not be confounded.

7 Unto you therefore which believe he is precious: but unto them which be disobedient, the stone which the builders disallowed, the same is made the head of the corner,

8 And a stone of stumbling, and a rock of offense, even to them which stumble at the word, being disobedient: whereunto also they were appointed.

9 But ye are a chosen generation, a royal priesthood, an holy nation, a peculiar people; that ye should show forth the praises of him who hath called you out of darkness into his marvelous light:

10 Which in time past were not a people, but are now the people of God: which had not obtained mercy, but now have obtained mercy.

1. God's new temple (vv. 4-8).—Psalm 118:22 reads, "The stone which the builders refused is become the head stone of the corner." In his speech before Jewish leaders, Peter referred this statement to the rejection of our Lord (Acts 4:10-11), as indeed Jesus Himself had done in Matthew 21:42. However, the major emphasis is not on humanity's rejection but God's approval and acceptance of Jesus, the "living stone," who is "chosen of God, and precious." He is the foundation stone in a new spiritual temple into which believers are built as "lively stones," providing not only "a spiritual house" but also "an holy priesthood." To all who regard Him as such Jesus is "precious," that is, of incomparable worth. To those who reject Him He is a "stone of stumbling," though they will eventually be forced to recognize Him as "the head of the corner."

2. Borrowed terms (vv. 9-10).—The four descriptive phrases in verse 9 are taken from Old Testament definitions of the nation Israel (Ex. 19:5-6). The word "peculiar" should be understood as meaning "cherished," as a prized personal possession. Once again, therefore, the idea of the church as successor to Israel is in view. Verse 10 echoes Hosea 1:10 and 2:23 where unfaithful Israel is replaced by others "which were not my people," foretelling the ingathering of the Gentiles and the establishment of the church. The idea of a "royal priesthood" is of special importance because it affirms the formation of a new priesthood to succeed that of Aaron and his sons. It furnishes the basis for the doctrine of the priesthood of believers, which not only implies the abolition of former priesthoods, but also repudiates the assumption of priestly functions and authority today. Under God's new covenant, all His people are priests having direct access to Him for themselves and are privileged to perform priestly services for others, not in an ecclesiastical sense but as advocates for others before God.

3. To the glory of God (v. 9b).—These privileges are not for self-gratification or advancement, but for the glory of God. As Christ, the chief "corner stone," was chosen of God (vv. 4-6), so also are those who make up a "chosen generation," believers who constitute the church. Israel of old was God's chosen people and is described as His "elect" (*chosen* and *elect* are the same word). Divine election has never been presented as a kind of favoritism by which certain people are given privileges above others. Rather, it is an appointment to service so that, while rejoicing in the benefits conferred on us as Christians, we can see these as reasons why we should minister to the needs of others, in Christ's name, thus bringing glory to our Benefactor.

III. Fulfilling Obligations (1 Pet. 2:11-25)

This idea continues to the end of the chapter and into the next as Peter mentioned areas of life into which the spirit of humble service should be carried. These are citizenship obligations, employee conduct, and family relationships (3:1-7). The historic context for these admonitions may differ from present conditions; for example, Peter wrote to slaves, but the principles have abiding value and importance.

1. As citizens (vv. 11-17).—Christianity had its beginning during times when oppression and persecution were prevalent. Believers' neighbors could be their next-door enemies, often basing their prejudiced attitudes on misinformation and misunderstanding. All kinds of false rumors were in circulation about Christians and their worship practices; thus, they became regarded as "evildoers" (v. 12). One effective answer to this was to be good citizens, for this would "put to silence the ignorance of foolish men" (v. 15). Christ's apostles consistently urged their followers to be law-abiding, cheerfully submitting to the many rules and regulations that were imposed by the Caesars and their representatives. This was not to mean violating the Christian's conscience by giving consent to things that one knew to be morally wrong or contrary to the laws of God. Over against Peter's advice in our current passage, we should recall what he said to the Jerusalem authorities when they tried to suppress the preaching of the gospel, "We ought to obey God rather than men" (Acts 5:29).

2. As workers (vv. 18-20).—In New Testament times, the slave population was in a ratio of one to five of the overall citizenry. The

Epistles indicate clearly that there were many slaves in the membership of the churches. The word translated "servants" both here and in other places refers to slaves. Some were captives of war, others debtors unable to meet their obligations. They included both the educated and the uneducated. As Christians, a potent witness to their faith could be borne by their attitude toward those who owned them. We can legitimately apply this teaching to employer-employee relationships today. The early messengers of Christ led no open opposition to the evils of slavery, except as they proclaimed the duty of mutual love, teaching that was eventually to eliminate slavery.

3. **As followers of Christ (vv. 21-25).**—In all the areas of life mentioned, and all others beside, the standard for our conduct is to be that of our Savior. His total selflessness caused Him to submit to death in our behalf, and He left "us an example, that [we] should follow his steps: . . . that we, being dead to sins, should live unto righteousness" (v. 21-24).

APPLYING THE LESSON

Desire to grow.—Pliny the Elder (A.D. 23-79) was a historian and scientist whose incurable curiosity has provided important details about daily life in ancient Rome. As a Roman military officer, he traveled all over the world. Everywhere he went, he recorded the geography, physics, and botany of the world he observed. His desire to learn led to both the fullness of his life and to his death. So curious was he and so desirous of learning that Pliny could not even take a bath without having some servant read to him so he could have some new fact to record in his journals later in the day. This desire for knowledge led to growth. It also led to his death. In A.D. 79, Pliny was meditating on a ship when he observed the first stages of the eruption of the volcano Mount Vesuvius. Instead of fleeing as others did, he moved his boat closer to get a better view, and he was eventually asphyxiated from the sulphurous gas that descended from the volcano.[1]

That same kind of curiosity and desire to learn was a part of the character of Simon Peter. That is why he grew from an uneducated fisherman to the gifted Christian whose Epistles are included in the text of Scripture.

Getting serious about God's Word.—Some of us are about the Bible like this little boy was. He wrote this letter to his pastor: "Dear Pastor, I've read the Bible every day since I was a little kid. So far I am up to the first page!" Like him, we often say we read the Bible but actually spend little time in God's Word.

Others of us are about the Bible like the famous outlaw of the old west, Jesse James. A minister who had known Jesse James in his earlier years bumped into him when he was in the midst of his life of crime. The minister reminded Jesse that he used to read the Bible when he was growing up. The outlaw immediately thrust his hand into his inside coat pocket and produced a

New Testament. The minister looked through the book in astonishment. It was marked up, showing constant use and frequent reading. Like Jesse James, we often read the Bible but do not follow the life-style it prescribes.

To grow spiritually, we must read the Bible, mark it, learn it, inwardly digest it, and then live by it. To those who approach the Bible in this way, the Bible is a resource Book that is never exhausted. A. T. Robertson, brilliant New Testament scholar, said late in his life, "Even after fifty years, I never open the Bible that I don't discover something new."

Church of preference.—A man was filling out a form on which he saw the words: "Church preference." He filled in the blank with the words: "Red Brick." Many times we think of the church in terms of buildings and structures. However, the essence of the church is people. Peter told us the church is made up of "living stones," that is, people who have built their lives on the "headstone of the corner."

All of us are priests.—We mark a sharp distinction today between laity and clergy. The New Testament describes all of us Christians in common terms. We are all saints. We are all believers. And we are all priests. Perhaps one dedicated Christian captured this thought when he was asked what he did for a living. He responded, "I am an ordained plumber." We are all ordained to be priests in God's new order.

What are you doing with your life?—Psychologist William Moulton Marston asked three thousand persons the question: "What are you living for?" Various answers were given, but the thrust of 94 percent of the answers was that these individuals were simply enduring the present, waiting for the future. They were waiting for something to happen. They were waiting for their children to grow up, or waiting until they could afford a trip, or waiting to get enough money to move to a new house, or waiting for someone to die, or waiting to retire. Their focus on tomorrow prevented them from fully experiencing today.

Christians must beware of that tendency. God promises a prepared place for His prepared people (John 14:1-3). God also has specific plans for His present people. We are not simply saved to enjoy the next life. We are saved to serve Christ in this life.

TEACHING THE CLASS

Main Idea: Believers are persons set apart in position and behavior by Christ.

Suggested Teaching Aim: Learners will describe their positions in Christ and the behavior expected of persons in that position.

Introduce the Bible Study

Display a picture of a child. Ask: How old would you guess the child to be? Elicit response. Continue: How would you feel if I told you this person is 42 years old? Elicit response. (Learners will probably respond with shock, sadness, and sympathy.) Ask rhetorically:

Would you agree this situation is representative of many followers of Jesus Christ? They are "old" in the faith but have not developed beyond the child level. Continue: Do we respond with equal dismay at this situation? Why?

State that the study for today focuses on the birth position of believers and their need to grow in behaviors that demonstrate who they are. Invite learners to open their Bibles to 1 Peter 2.

Search for Biblical Truth

Share the comments titled "Desire to grow" (*Applying the Lesson*). State that Peter placed emphasis on the reason for growth within believers. Call on a learner to read 1 Peter 2:1-3 while other learners listen to discover the reason believers should want to grow. When the reading is finished, call for response. (See v. 3.)

A Teaching Outline
1. Focus on personal growth.
2. Discover the reason for commitment to grow as Christians.
3. State some things to do that can produce Christian growth and development.
4. Commit themselves to growth in Christ.

Continue by asking: What things are cited as inhibitors of growth in the believer? (See v. 1.) List responses on the chalkboard.

Direct learners to discuss the meaning of each of the words on the chalkboard with those sitting near them. After a few minutes, discuss the words with the group.

Continue with the question: What will produce growth in believers? (See v. 2.) Elicit response. Continue: What is the meaning of the phrase "the sincere milk of the word"? Use the comments titled "Getting serious about God's Word" (*Applying the Lesson*).

Note that Peter turned to comment on the basis of believers growth in Christian qualities. Call on a learner to read 1 Peter 2:4-8 aloud from a modern translation. When finished, ask: What is the basis from which believers can grow in Christian qualities? (Their position in Christ.)

Direct learners to read verse 5 again to themselves. Share the comments titled "All of us are priests" (*Applying the Lesson*).

Note that verses 9 and 10 reiterate the special position of believers in Christ. Call on a learner to read them aloud. Write the four descriptive phrases from these verses on the chalkboard. Direct learners to discuss the meaning of each phrase with those sitting near them. After a few minutes, discuss the concepts with the larger group. Conclude by asking: What is the purpose of believers having this special position? (See v. 9b.)

Give the Truth a Personal Focus

Share the comments titled "What are you doing with your life? (*Applying the Lesson*). Ask: How many of us would choose to be a 42-year-old infant? Would we choose to be a 42-year-old spiritual infant? Allow a moment for learners to consider this choice.

Continue by asking: How can we prevent stunted growth as a believer? What are some things to do that produce Christian growth and development? Elicit response.

Challenge learners to commit themselves to growth based on their positions in Christ.

---

1. Malcolm Forbes, *They Went That a Way,* 237.

May 10

Witness in the Midst of Suffering

Basic Passage: 1 Peter 3:13—4:11

Focal Passages: 1 Peter 3:13-18; 4:1-2,7-11

Our lesson title could cause some of us to react: This is not for me, though I recognize it may have application to others. An important question, therefore, is: Was Peter referring to persecution already existing or to a looming probability? The tense of his verbs suggests the latter. The recurring word "if" also supports this. At the same time, Peter's readers were already experiencing opposition in the form of verbal abuse. We know from history that this abuse changed to violent hostility. This condition exists in some parts of the world today, so this lesson should stimulate our prayers for fellow believers who are paying a high price for their loyalty to Christ. Many feel that seeds of hostility are being sown in our own country where biblical values are under attack and those who hold to them are held up to ridicule and contempt. Therefore this study may challenge us to evaluate our relationship with a secular, sometimes godless, culture and force us to ask: If the cost of Christian discipleship should rise, where would I stand?

Study Aim: *To induce prayerful concern for all who suffer for Christ's sake and test our own willingness to pay that price*

STUDYING THE BIBLE

Peter wrote in desperate times. If some of his standards seem extreme (3:1-12), we should realize that they were matched to conditions in which it was of supreme importance for a clear line to be drawn between persons who made profession of faith in Christ and those who did not. Do present conditions require less exacting standards for those who confess Jesus as Lord?

I. Suffering for Righteousness' Sake (1 Pet. 3:13-18)

There is no chapter division between 3:12 and 13 though there might well be. Peter had been discussing the behavior of Christians, and their relationship to one another, concluding with the statement, "For the eyes of the Lord are over the righteous, . . . but the face of the Lord is against them that do evil" (v. 12). Then he abruptly changed themes, suggesting that he was responding to news that had just reached him, even as he wrote. Did that news concern a rising tide of opposition to the gospel and its adherents?

> 13 And who is he that will harm you, if ye be followers of that which is good?
> 14 But and if ye suffer for righteousness' sake, happy are ye: and be not afraid of their terror, neither be troubled;
> 15 But sanctify the Lord God in your hearts: and be ready always to give an answer to every man that asketh you a reason of the hope that is in you with meekness and fear:
> 16 Having a good conscience; that, whereas they speak evil of you, as of evildoers, they may be ashamed that falsely accuse your good conversation in Christ.
> 17 For it is better, if the will of God be so, that ye suffer for welldoing, than for evildoing.
> 18 For Christ also hath once suffered for sins, the just for the unjust, that he might bring us to God, being put to death in the flesh, but quickened by the Spirit.

1. Divine protection (vv. 13-14).—We are reminded of Paul's question, "If God be for us, who can be against us?" (Rom. 8:31). Such questions should not encourage any pollyannaish attitude toward pain and suffering. Rather, they are an assurance that if hostility should take an extreme form so that lives are forfeited, believers are only hastened thereby into the presence of their Lord, whereas their foes must face the justice of God (4:5).

2. Loyalty to Christ (v. 15).—Another reading is: "In your hearts reverence Christ as Lord" (RSV). The right answer to persecution is not retreat but fresh commitment to the lordship of Christ, which demands a loyalty that exceeds all others. Opposition should be made an opportunity for witness to one's personal faith. That witness should be borne in a humble spirit. Well-intentioned aggressiveness on the part of witnessing Christians can become an obstacle to positive response and may even deepen hostility. Thus it should be avoided.

3. Guarded behavior (vv. 16-17).—The word *conversation* means manner of life. Hatred toward Christians expressed itself in slander as they were falsely accused of unlawful and even immoral behavior. Peter's advice was, "Keep your conscience clear" (NRSV)—that is, no matter what people may say, see to it that their accusations are not true. If you have to suffer, it is better to do so for the good that you do and not the evil.

4. The supreme Sufferer (v. 18).—Our Savior suffered more than any of His followers. Though without sin ("just"), He died for sinners ("the unjust"); His purpose was to make it possible for unrighteous persons to be reconciled to God. (Verses 19-22, though in our basic material, are of uncertain meaning. One commentator records finding over thirty different interpretations. We shall serve our present purpose best by acknowledging the problem and leaving it unsolved.)

II. Following Christ's Example (1 Pet. 4:1-6)

We cannot but be impressed by the way Peter repeatedly presents our Lord as both Savior and Example. This is the man who, when Jesus broke the news of His coming death, responded with, "Be it far from thee, Lord: this shall not be unto thee" (Matt. 16:22). He had now become a fervent preacher of the crucified Christ, "Who his own self bare our sins in his own body on the tree, that we, being dead to sins, should live unto righteousness" (2:24).

> 1 Forasmuch then as Christ hath suffered for us in the flesh, arm yourselves likewise with the same mind: for he that hath suffered in the flesh hath ceased from sin;
> 2 That he no longer should live the rest of his time in the flesh to the lusts of men, but to the will of God.

1. The mind of Christ (v. 1).—Our Lord's example of vicarious suffering ("for us") is again offered as a pattern for the believer. Not that we should welcome suffering in general, but suffering that is for His sake and therefore honorable and redemptive. We are to "arm" ourselves with the mind of our Master, being willing to face the consequences of our loyalty to Him. Perhaps Peter used this military term because such an attitude has protective values against the onslaught of sin. To be fully committed to Christ will liberate us from evil influences so that it may be said of us that we have "ceased from sin," not sinless but no longer dominated by sin.

2. A vital choice (vv. 2-3).—These words suggest a Gentile readership rather than a Jewish, for they describe a pagan life-style that includes "idolatries." Dedication to a Christian manner of life, that may include suffering for Christ's sake, demands a complete separation from the past with its evil ways. The temptation to compromise is ever present, and only a firm purpose set on doing "the will of God" can keep us from faltering.

3. Weapons of words (vv. 4-5).—Former associates in sin may become a Christian's worst enemies. Their unregenerate minds are unable to understand the changes that have taken place in you. Therefore they become abusive. In the first Christian century, believers were slandered with a variety of false accusations. Those responsible would eventually have to face judgment from the Lord whom they maligned, for the "him" in verse 5 appears to refer to the Lord Jesus who will "judge the quick [living] and the dead at his appearing and his kingdom" (2 Tim. 4:1).

III. The Hope that Sustains (1 Pet. 4:7-11)

Included in the basic doctrine of New Testament believers was the coming again of the Lord Jesus. This doctrine is rooted in the Old Testament, which describes the Messiah in terms that were not fulfilled during His life on earth as God's incarnate Son. The Gospels contain many references to His return, statements made for the most part by Jesus Himself. Apostles taught their converts to be expectant of His return and encouraged the belief that this might happen during their life time. This was the hope that sustained a persecuted people even when faced by martyrdom.

> 7 But the end of all things is at hand: be ye therefore sober, and watch unto prayer.
> 8 And above all things have fervent charity among yourselves: for charity shall cover the multitude of sins.
> 9 Use hospitality one to another without grudging.
> 10 As every man hath received the gift, even so minister the same one to another, as good stewards of the manifold grace of God.
> 11 If any man speak, let him speak as the oracles of God; if any man minister, let him do it as of the ability that God giveth: that

God in all things may be glorified through Jesus Christ, to whom be praise and dominion forever and ever. Amen.

1. The approaching end (v. 7a).—The Lord did not come in the first Christian century. Interestingly enough, it is Peter who is credited with explaining this, a subject we will take up on May 31. But when every explanation has been offered, the fact remains that believers of every century, including the present, should live expecting Christ's appearing.

2. Consequences in life (vv. 7b-9).—The effect of this hope can be disciplined ("be ye therefore sober"), prayerful behavior. Moreover, it should induce mutual love expressed in such ways as gracious hospitality. The more outside pressures increased, the more important it was for the Christian community to live and work together in harmony. The final statement of verse 8 means that when love abounds, criticism is suppressed as the faults and failings of others are forced into the background.

3. Humble sharing (vv. 10-11).—Apostolic teaching was in agreement. Paul taught that as members of one body believers should share their God-given abilities, using them humbly for the benefit of all (1 Cor. 12). Peter presented a similar idea, "Like good stewards of the manifold grace of God, serve one another with whatever gift each of you has received. . . . whoever serves must do so with the strength that God supplies, so that God may be glorified in all things through Jesus Christ" (NRSV). God's glory, not our own, is to be the objective of all Christian service.

APPLYING THE LESSON

Looking for trouble.—A wife woke up her husband in the middle of the night. "Someone is in the house," she whispered. To satisfy her, the husband went downstairs to look around. When he turned the lights on, he found himself face-to-face with a burglar. The burglar put a gun in the man's face and told him if he kept quiet he would not be hurt. The man told the burglar he had no intention of giving him trouble. But then he added, "I do have a favor to ask you. I wish you would wait here until I bring my wife down. I want you to meet her because she has been looking for you from time to time for twenty years."

Some people go through life looking for trouble. Truth is, we do not have to look very far to find trouble, for suffering of some kind is a part of the life experience of every person. Peter wrote about the kind of suffering that comes specifically because of our faith in Christ.

Quit playing around.—Dr. Morris Townsend dedicated his life to the cause of Christ as a physician and had to endure through many experiences of suffering and difficulty. Through it all, he remained faithful to the Lord. He was asked to share his experience and his faith at Keswick, a gathering for Christians, but was unable to fulfill the commitment because of poor health. Instead, he wrote this letter to Radcliffe Allen who had asked him to speak: "Dear Brother Allen: I had been looking forward to this, but I was restrained from getting in touch with you because I have something more important to look forward to. It has pleased God in His sovereignty to put cancer in both my lungs and in my liver, and it is the fast spreading type. So in all probability I will be in the presence of my Lord before next October." In the midst of this rather long letter, the key phrase was a challenge Dr. Townsend gave. He said, "Please convey to all the men this message: 'Stop playing around with Christianity.'"[1]

That is a good summary statement of the message of Peter's epistle. Great difficulties must be countered with great dedication.

What did you do about the boy?—Warren Cranford went to Africa on a missionary venture. He made slides while he was there and used these slides in his first presentation to a church when he came back home. On one of the slides was a little African boy. He had his nose and his hands pressed up tightly against the bakery window. Cranford went around inside the bakery and captured the expression of this little boy with his nose and hands against the window. Above his head was the sign: "Bakery." Cranford ended his slide presentation with the picture of this boy. When he asked for questions, someone in the congregation asked, "What did you do about the boy?" For the first time, Cranford realized that he had simply taken the picture of the boy, then walked away and done nothing.

All around us are "boys" like that one who need food and to hear a word about Christ. Our responsibility as Christians is to give a testimony to others about the faith that is within us.

A picture of the cross.—One of the great hymns of our faith is "When I Survey the Wondrous Cross." Like so many of our enduring hymns, the impact is made by the words of the text. Study the words of the hymn. Perhaps, you could even have your class sing the hymn. Then point out the theological truths that the hymn presents about Jesus. We see Jesus as a great Savior (v. 1) and as one who confronted a great sin (v. 3). In addition, we see that the only proper response to such a Savior is a great sacrifice (v. 2) and a complete surrender (v. 4).

A change demanded.—Alexander the Great was a conqueror who demanded unquestioned allegiance from his men. One day he heard of a soldier who had retreated instead of meeting the enemy. The man's name was the same as that of the great conqueror. Alexander the Great confronted the man. "Is your name Alexander?" he asked. "Yes," the soldier replied. "And did you retreat in the heat of the battle?" "Yes," the soldier answered. Alexander the Great retorted, "Then, young man, you need to either change your name or change your actions!"

To be a Christian means to be like Christ. If we are not willing to follow His example, we do not need to call ourselves by His name.

MAY 10, 1992

TEACHING THE CLASS

Main Idea: Believers are to live in love and prayer when suffering comes.

Suggested Teaching Aim: Learners will pray for power to live in love in the midst of suffering.

Introduce the Bible Study

Share the comments titled "Looking for trouble" (*Applying the Lesson*). State that for most of us looking for trouble, problems, hard times, and suffering is not necessary. If we live long enough, we will experience some of it. Ask: How do you handle it? Does being a believer make a difference in the way you handle life's pains? Elicit response.

Note that the study for today focuses on Peter's instructions to people who were experiencing serious suffering. Invite learners to open their Bibles to 1 Peter 3.

Search for Biblical Truth

Use information from *Studying the Bible* to describe the difficult times in which Peter wrote these words. Direct learners to scan 1 Peter 3:13-18 to locate words that indicate the level of difficulty these believers were experiencing. After a few minutes, call for response.

A Teaching Outline
1. Introduce the problem of suffering.
2. Review Peter's discussion of suffering in lives of believers.
3. Identify behavior appropriate for periods of suffering.
4. Pray for power to act in love in the midst of suffering.

Call on a learner to read 1 Peter 3:13-18 aloud while others listen to discover what believers were instructed to do in these circumstances. Call for response. Note them on the chalkboard. Responses should include the following: don't be afraid, don't be troubled, focus on the Lord, give an explanation for your behavior in humility, have a good conscience.

Refer to verse 18. Ask: What pattern do believers have to follow? Wait for response. Note that 1 Peter 4 continues this same thought. Call on someone to read 1 Peter 4:1-2. Ask: What is the good outcome of suffering?

Note that 1 Peter 4:7-11 gives some specific instructions about what believers are to do while living in difficult times. Direct learners to read the verses to themselves and be ready to state those behaviors. Call for response. Write responses on the chalkboard. They should include be prayerful, be serious about life, love fervently, be hospitable to others, give generously of what you have, speak for God, and minister in God's name. When the listing is finished, ask: What is the purpose of this behavior? After their response remark that the purpose is not to stop the suffering but to glorify God in it. Share the comments titled "Quit playing around" (*Applying the Lesson*).

Give the Truth a Personal Focus

Share the comments titled "What did you do about the boy" (*Applying the Lesson*). Explain that to know what should be done is not the point, but to decide how to do what should be done and then do it is the point.

Provide paper and pens. Direct learners to think of difficulties that they face. Perhaps the difficulties are financial problems, family problems, work problems, or spiritual problems. Help them to focus on the difficult times in their current lives. Direct them to consider the behavior listed on the chalkboard and privately complete this open-ended sentence: In this tough situation, I will ___trust GOD___.

Allow several minutes for learners to complete this work.

Conclude the study with the comments titled "A change demanded" from *Applying the Lesson.* Spend several minutes praying together for power to act in love in the midst of suffering.

---

1. A. Dudley Dennison, *Prescription for Life: Medicinal and Spiritual Perspectives on Your Personal Needs* (Grand Rapids: Zondervan Publishing House, 1975), 71.

May 17

Humble, Steadfast, Vigilant

Basic Passage: 1 Peter 5:1-11

Focal Passage: 1 Peter 5:1-11

While opposition to Christ and His gospel increased, the churches continued to function as centers for worship, fellowship, and witness. One of the values of New Testament epistles is the light they shed on conditions in these first-century churches. We would like to think of those conditions as ideal, but human nature was the same then as it is today; and Christians are not immune to selfish interests, though when they give way to them they repudiate the high standards of personal conduct that their faith imposes. Peter wrote, with a deep sense of urgency, to correct trends that if not resisted could do serious damage to the progress of the gospel. That he addressed himself to "elders" and "ye younger," as distinct categories within the church, should remind us that first-century culture was different from ours. Leadership was then reserved for older people, whereas today youth are playing a growing part in most areas of life. Yet the principles of behavior laid down by the apostle are as valid now as they were then.

Study Aim: *To evaluate responsibilities and relationships within the church and enlist all concerned in resisting evil*

STUDYING THE BIBLE

Peter possessed qualifications to write this chapter that were superior to most. He was among the first disciples (John 1:40-42) and belonged to the small intimate group that witnessed the transfiguration and other significant events in our Lord's life (Mark 9:2; 14:33). Peter led the others in acknowledging Jesus as Messiah (8:29), and he was first to enter the open and empty sepulcher (John 20:6). He became spokesman for the infant church on the day of Pentecost (Acts 2:14), and he was one of the leaders in the Jerusalem church (Gal. 1:18-19), which recognized him as apostle to the Jews (2:8). Christian tradition holds that he suffered martyrdom in Rome.

55

I. Advice for Leaders (1 Pet. 5:1-4)

The office of elder has frequent mention in the New Testament. Paul and Barnabas "ordained them elders in every church" after their missionary tour of Asia Minor (Acts 14:23). On his final journey to Jerusalem, Paul summoned the elders of the church in Ephesus to whom he said, "Take heed . . . unto yourselves, and to all the flock, over the which the Holy Ghost hath made you overseers, to feed the church of God" (Acts 20:28). How these elders related to other church officials we do not know. It is possible that "elder" and "bishop" are interchangeable terms.

> 1 The elders which are among you I exhort, who am also an elder, and a witness of the sufferings of Christ, and also a partaker of the glory that shall be revealed:
> 2 Feed the flock of God which is among you, taking the oversight thereof, not by constraint, but willingly; not for filthy lucre, but of a ready mind;
> 3 Neither as being lords over God's heritage, but being examples to the flock.
> 4 And when the chief Shepherd shall appear, ye shall receive a crown of glory that fadeth not away.

Nothing in Scripture indicates Peter held office in a local church, apart from Jerusalem where he functioned as an apostle. Perhaps he considered the lesser office to be combined with the greater. In any case, he showed humility of spirit by describing himself as "also an elder," a humility that he enjoined on his readers. However, Peter claimed great privileges, namely, to have witnessed both Christ's sufferings and glory, the latter a probable reference to the transfiguration. He urged elders, "Feed the flock of God," which compares with Paul's words already quoted. Their ministry should be "not under compulsion but willingly, . . . not for sordid gain but eagerly. Do not lord it over those in your charge, but be examples to the flock" (NRSV). It would seem that these exhortations to humble, selfless service are needed today. The only reward to be sought is "a crown . . . that fadeth not away," not a royal crown but one of laurel that, unlike those bestowed on successful athletes, will prove imperishable. Those who prove themselves good undershepherds will be thus acknowledged by "the chief Shepherd."

II. Counsel for Followers (1 Pet. 5:5-7)

Whether "elder" is used in the same sense as "elders" in verse 1 is open to question. Here it may just mean older Christians, although this use would certainly include those previously described as "elders." The call to mutual subjection has a parallel in the apostle Paul's counsel to husbands and wives. While writing that "the husband is head of the wife," Paul also wrote, "Submitting yourselves one to another in the fear of God" (Eph. 5:21). Leadership is necessary in all areas of life, but it is to be compassionate and open to reasoning, so that the relationship is cordial, and not conflicting. The Greek for "be clothed with humility" literally means "put on the apron of humility" and therefore appears to relate to the incident recorded in John 13:1-17 in which Peter played a conspicuous part. As Jesus "took a towel, and girded himself," so all Christians, both young and old, are to render humble service to one another.

> 5 Likewise, ye younger, submit yourselves unto the elder. Yea, all of you be subject one to another, and be clothed with humility: for God resisteth the proud, and giveth grace to the humble.
> 6 Humble yourselves therefore under the mighty hand of God, that he may exalt you in due time:
> 7 Casting all your care upon him; for he careth for you.

The exhortation of verse 6 probably relates to the hardships Christians were undergoing at that time. God was not the cause of their hardships, but He was permitting them for an unstated purpose. The right attitude toward them was humble acceptance in the knowledge that God was in control, and He would bring His people out of their distresses "in due time." In the meantime, they should cast all their "anxiety" (NRSV), or worries, on Him "for he careth for you."

III. Dealing with the Adversary (1 Pet. 5:8-9)

The counsel of 4:7 is repeated as Peter called for disciplined living and vigilance, only here the vigilance is to be directed toward the activities of "your adversary the devil." More to be feared than any earthly foe, even than the imperial power of Rome, was Satan. He is compared to "a roaring lion," always on the prowl to catch and destroy the unwary. Effective protection against this enemy could be found in being "steadfast in the faith," that is, to exercise total and unwavering commitment to, and trust in, God. Others, they needed to remember, were experiencing the same pressures and offering the same resistance (v. 9b). A need for us today, if the profession and practice of our faith is not exposing us to abuse, is to have in mind those who are suffering for Christ's sake. A Christian publication has stated that in this century an average of 300,000 believers have been martyred each year.[1]

> 8 Be sober, be vigilant; because your adversary the devil, as a roaring lion, walketh about, seeking whom he may devour:

9 Whom resist steadfast in the faith, knowing that the same afflictions are accomplished in your brethren that are in the world.

Peter's imperatives should be noted: "Feed" (v. 2), "submit" (v. 5), "cast" (v. 7, NRSV), "Be sober, be vigilant" (v. 8), and "resist" (v. 9) are in agreement with Paul's exhortation to "work out" our salvation (Phil. 2:12). We can do nothing to earn salvation, which is God's free gift. But in the power of the Holy Spirit, our wills can (and should) cooperate with the purpose of God in our lives. To make a profession of faith, and then assume there is nothing more for us to do, is a grave misunderstanding. There are goals to be gained and battles to be won that demand the utmost of our efforts, made in the strength that God supplies.

IV. Facing the Future (1 Pet. 5:10-11)

Salvation begins and ends with God. For all Christians, there are crises along the way that occasion the question: "Will I ever make it?" Imagine what it was for these early believers who had to contend with the devil's schemes (as do we all), plus the animosity of unbelievers, and the cruel attacks of the civil authorities. Verse 10 reads like a prayer in the KJV, but in other versions it is a statement of confident hope as it affirms that God *will* do these things.

> **10** But the God of all grace, who hath called us unto his eternal glory by Christ Jesus, after that ye have suffered a while, make you perfect, stablish, strengthen, settle you.
> **11** To him be glory and dominion forever and ever. Amen.

Trouble is easier to bear when an end to it is in sight. Peter could assure his readers that there was an end, and that it would come "after . . . a while." The God who gives grace to bear tribulation is also the source, through Jesus Christ, of a call to enjoy His "eternal glory." When that time comes, said the apostle, He "will himself restore, support, strengthen, and establish you" (NRSV). No wonder he concluded with a doxology (v. 11).

V. Some Final Words (1 Pet. 5:12-14)

We would not want to leave this powerful letter without a glance at how it concludes. It was written, at Peter's dictation, by a "faithful brother" named Silvanus. This was the Silas of Acts 15:22, whom Paul, after his disagreement with Barnabas, chose as companion on his second missionary journey (v. 40). The tribute paid here indicates that Silas was a man of stature in the New Testament churches and may have contributed the high literary style that is recognizable in 1 Peter. The greeting from the "church that is at Babylon" (v. 13) raises the question of where this epistle was written. Wherever it was, a church existed there (v. 13), and this would appear to rule out the ancient city of that name in Mesopotamia. Historic sources tell that this city was abandoned by its Jewish community around the middle of the first Christian century. A later writer tells of the city being in ruins some sixty years later. A reasonable assumption is that Peter used the name Babylon for Rome, which had become the enemy of the church just as ancient Babylon was the enemy of Israel. We note with interest that Mark was another companion of Peter at that time.

APPLYING THE LESSON

The purpose of leadership.—What is a leader to do? Volumes have been written in answer to that question. Cut through the verbiage, and you can summarize the answers with two words: example and encouragement. A leader is to provide an example of what needs to be done. Then, he or she is to encourage others as they move in that direction. What a difference we would see in our churches today if leaders would do what leaders are supposed to do.

Faithfulness to the task.—One of the primary requirements of a preacher is faithfulness. No one better exemplified that than Charles Simeon. Born in 1759, he was converted as an undergraduate at Cambridge and longed to have an opportunity to preach there. When he walked by the Holy Trinity Church on the Cambridge campus, he would say to himself, "How I would rejoice if God gave me the opportunity to preach the gospel in this church." God answered his prayer, and in 1872, Simeon became the pastor of the church. The joy of the experience quickly evaporated in the face of stringent opposition from the people. The longtime members of the church who owned the seats, as was custom in those days, boycotted the services and locked the doors to their pews. For more than ten years the congregation had to stand. But Simeon persevered and gradually earned the respect of the town and the campus. For fifty-four years he remained at the church, teaching the Bible in a systematic way and giving exemplary leadership to the people.[2] Charles Simeon is a model of the kind of pastor Peter described in our text.

Two types of humility.—One writer described two kinds of humility and labeled them: Humility Type 1 and Humility Type 2. Humility Type 1 is described in Romans 12:3 and simply means not thinking more of ourselves than we ought to think, that is, having a right perspective about ourselves. Such humility does not mean to think little of ourselves. It simply means to think properly of ourselves. Humility Type 2 is a kind of self-debasement that causes us to miss completely the strengths and value that we do have. This kind of humility usually comes from comparing ourselves to others. Such self-debasement often leads to envy of spirit toward others.[3]

The kind of humility Peter recommended in our text is Humility Type 1, which comes from a proper perspective of God and a proper perspective of ourselves. When we look at God, we recognize that He is the source and strength of our lives. When we look at ourselves, we realize that we do have value, but only because of what God does for us and through us.

The devil's beatitudes.—Peter's mention of the devil, whose purpose is to undermine the work of God and to discourage the people of God, should alert us to the importance of the devil's beatitudes.

Blessed are they that are too tired and busy to go to church on Sunday, for they are my best workers. Blessed are they who are bored with the minister's mannerisms and mistakes, for they get nothing out of the sermon. Blessed is the church member who expects to be invited to his own church, for he is an important member to me. Blessed are they who do not go to church on Sunday evening, for they cause the world to say the church is failing. Blessed are they who gossip, for they cause strife and divisions that please me very much. Blessed are they who are easily offended, for they soon get angry and quit. Blessed are they who do not give their tithes and offerings to carry on God's work, for they are my helpers. Blessed are they who profess to love God but hate their brothers, for they shall be with me forever. Blessed are the troublemakers, for they shall be called the children of the devil. Blessed are they who have no time to pray, for they will be easy prey.

Hope helps us cope.—An executive took early retirement with this explanation, "For thirty years I have been coping with people, and I have run out of cope." Many of us come to situations in life when we feel like that. For the Christian, our hope in Christ helps us to cope. Our hope is rooted in what Christ did. Because He lived on this earth and faced the same things we face, we know He understands our situation. Because He won victory over the things we face, we know that He can enable us to win the victory as well.

TEACHING THE CLASS

Main Idea: Believers have leadership and "followship" responsibilities.

Suggested Teaching Aim: Learners will determine appropriate qualities and activities for leaders and followers.

Introduce the Bible Study

Write the following on the chalkboard: *lead, follow, or get out of the way.* Note that while this is not a Christian guideline, it communicates effectively.

Ask: Why do we need leaders? Why do we need followers? After their response, share the comments titled "The purpose of leadership" from *Applying the Lesson.*

Note that the Bible gives instructions about both the role of the leader and the follower and that Peter's writings comment about them. Invite learners to open their Bibles to 1 Peter 5.

Search for Biblical Truth

Share information from *Studying the Bible* to provide the setting from which these words were written. Display the following outline to guide the study of this chapter.

> Leaders, Followers
> 1 Peter 5:1-11
> 1. Advice for leaders (vv. 1-4)
> 2. Counsel for followers (vv. 5-7)
> 3. Dealing with the adversary (vv. 8-9)
> 4. Facing the future (vv. 10-11)
> 5. Some final words (vv. 12-14)

Assign the five sections of the Scripture to groups of learners. Direct them to study the passage and be prepared to tell what advice or counsel on how to deal with the adversary, how to face the future, or final words Peter had to share. Allow several minutes for study and discussion.

A Teaching Outline
1. Consider the place of leaders and followers.
2. Discover biblical instructions concerning both roles.
3. Determine how to follow the biblical instructions in their lives.

When the study is finished, call on a learner to read the entire chapter aloud from a modern translation. Guide a discussion with questions like the following:

What advice does Peter have for leaders? Share the comments titled "Faithfulness to the task" (*Applying the Lesson*). Ask: What is the reward of a leader?

What counsel does Peter have for followers? Share the comments titled "Two types of humility" (*Applying the Lesson*). Ask: What is the reward of the follower?

How did Peter advise readers to deal with the devil? Share the comments titled "The devil's beatitudes" (*Applying the Lesson*).

How are believers to face the future? Share the comments titled "Hope helps us cope" (*Applying the Lesson*). Ask: What is the reward of those who face the future with hope?

What final words did Peter have in this letter? Share information from *Studying the Bible* to supplement response.

Give the Truth a Personal Focus

Ask: Would you consider yourself a leader or a follower in most areas of your life? Allow a moment for learners to consider their position. Direct learners to review the Scripture that applies to the position they most often take and consider the instructions from Peter. Allow several minutes for reflection.

Ask rhetorically: What specific behavior in your role would reflect these principles? Encourage learners to visualize themselves acting in the way Peter described. Conclude the study with a prayer of commitment to live out these principles in their lives.

---

1. *Christianity Today*, March 19, 1990, 12.
2. John R. W. Stott, *Between Two Worlds* (Grand Rapids: Wm. B. Eerdmans Publishing Co., 1982), 33.
3. Patrick Morley, *The Man in the Mirror*, 191.

May 24

Growing In Grace

Basic Passage: 2 Peter 1:1-14

Focal Passage: 2 Peter 1:1-14

The second letter that bears Peter's name was written to Christians exposed to false doctrine. It has three major themes: warning against heretical teaching, affirmation of the hope of the Lord's return, and exhortation to spiritual growth. The error pinpointed in this letter is gnosticism, from the Greek word for knowledge. Gnostics taught, among other things, that the way to salvation is through knowledge. From other New Testament books we know that early forms of gnosticism troubled the churches of the first Christian century, though true gnosticism did not develop till later. But the situation was serious enough for the apostle John to write against it, and 2 Peter contends with the same doctrinal enemy. This brief letter recommends growth in grace (2 Pet. 3:18) as protection against false teaching, and its recommendation is valid against every form of error, both then and now. Undeveloped and uninformed Christians are fair prey to purveyors of unbiblical ideas. Hence the importance of Christian education, including the Sunday School.

[Margin note: Good Thought]

Study Aim: *To recognize spiritual maturity, and deepening understanding of biblical truth, as protection against error*

STUDYING THE BIBLE

The phrase, "cunningly devised fables" (v. 16), refers to another aspect of false teaching, namely, misrepresenting the person of Christ and His mission as Savior. In 2:1, charges are brought against "false teachers . . . even denying the Lord that bought them." The persistence of such teaching today makes this epistle relevant to our times so that we should take careful note of its counsel on how to resist its influence and stand strong in the faith.

I. A Believer's Privileges (2 Pet. 1:1-4)

Peter began his letter with a strong statement on the Christian's standing before God and its corresponding responsibilities. He wrote to those who shared with him "like precious faith" (v. 1). The unusual phrase, "of God and our Savior Jesus Christ," could have been directed against those who denied the unique relationship between the Father and the Son. Our shared faith is centered in One who, though being very God, laid aside His heavenly glory and assumed human flesh that He might become our Redeemer. The basis of our faith can be tested by our answer to the question, "What think ye of Christ? whose son is he?" (Matt. 22:42).

> **1** Simon Peter, a servant and an apostle of Jesus Christ, to them that have obtained like precious faith with us through the righteousness of God and our Savior Jesus Christ:
> **2** Grace and peace be multiplied unto you through the knowledge of God, and of Jesus our Lord,
> **3** According as his divine power hath given unto us all things that pertain unto life and godliness, through the knowledge of him that hath called us to glory and virtue:
> **4** Whereby are given unto us exceeding great and precious promises: that by these ye might be partakers of the divine nature, having escaped the corruption that is in the world through lust.

1. Knowledge available (v. 2).—Two references to knowledge in as many verses (2 and 3) are worthy of note. Persons who bragged about their superior knowledge, and the spiritual advantages it brought, caused others to feel inferior. Such reaction is unjustified since knowledge of the right sort is available to every believer, that is, "knowledge of God, and of Jesus our Lord."

2. Provision made (v. 3).—Emphasis continues on the adequacy of God's provision for those who seek this true knowledge, "all things that pertain unto life and godliness" covering every requirement for both physical and spiritual life. There was no need for Peter's readers to go seeking fuller revelations. All they needed was available to them in Christ who calls His people to "glory and goodness" (NRSV), that is, to share in His own nature.

3. Promises given (v. 4a).—God's people have always lived in reliance on divine promises. The hope of a coming Messiah inspired Old Testament saints with its prospect of better times to come. New Testament believers are also recipients of glorious promises for themselves (heaven and eternal life) and for the church (our Lord's return and the establishment of His kingdom). There are also "great and precious promises" that sustain us in times of trouble.

4. Relationship established (v. 4b).—A promise fulfilled for the believer is adoption into the family of God becomes a reality through faith in Christ. What a change this involves, for we are delivered from "the corruption that is in the world" and made recipients of the divine nature! The claim is stupendous, but it is in line with John's teaching, "Behold, what manner of love the Father hath bestowed upon us, that we should be called the sons of God" (1 John 3:1).

II. A Believer's Responsibilities (2 Pet. 1:5-7)

The phrase "beside this" obscures the true meaning, which is, "For this very reason" (NRSV). The Christian's high privileges provide the reason to "make every effort" (NRSV) to build on faith a life-style that is pleasing to God and a blessing to one's fellows. Eight qualities are named. (Eight is the number of notes in a musical octave and suggests a life in harmony with God's will.) All are essential, so we are not offered a cafeteria choice from which to pick our preferences but the essential ingredients of a well-rounded Christian character.

> 5 And beside this, giving all diligence, add to your faith virtue; and to virtue knowledge;
> 6 And to knowledge temperance; and to temperance patience; and to patience godliness;
> 7 And to godliness brotherly kindness; and to brotherly kindness charity.

1. Incentive and response (v. 5a).—The opening words of this verse look back over all that precedes them and argues that because of all the blessings conferred on believers, they are obligated to play their part in developing a nature that is in accord with their high standing in Christ. As "partakers of the divine nature," we are to see to it that character and conduct reflect this amazing relationship. And we are to do it with "all diligence," directing our total effort toward attaining these goals.

2. **Eight Christian qualities (vv. 5b-7).**—They are founded in faith and crowned with love ("charity"). Faith is the indispensable starting point, because these are qualities impossible to attain apart from God's help. *Virtue* is a strong word suggesting courageous uprightness. *Knowledge* is not offered as a way to salvation but to living life at its best. For us, a growing understanding of God's way and will must come from study of the Scriptures. *Temperance* means "self-discipline," not a favorite subject with the gnostics or the pagans of those times who were more inclined to doing "what comes naturally." *Patience* should be understood as "endurance" or "steadfastness." Temptation to quit under pressure was strong but must be resisted. *Godliness* may be contrasted with "ungodly" (3:7). It describes a right attitude toward God so that fellowship with Him is deepened and strengthened. Prayer, Bible reading, and worship are necessary aids. *Brotherly kindness* refers to relationships within the church, while charity (*agape* love) is to be shown to all persons.

III. A Believer's Prospects (2 Pet. 1:8-14)

To possess faith without these qualities is to be an anemic Christian whose life will make little impression on others. Many who say, "I believe in God," or, "Yes, I have been saved," show little evidence in their lives. It is for this evidence that Peter pleads. Faith is tremendously important, but it should be regarded as the starting point for Christian living.

> 8 For if these things be in you, and abound, they make you that ye shall neither be barren nor unfruitful in the knowledge of our Lord Jesus Christ.
> 9 But he that lacketh these things is blind, and cannot see afar off, and hath forgotten that he was purged from his old sins.
> 10 Wherefore the rather, brethren, give diligence to make your calling and election sure: for if ye do these things, ye shall never fall:
> 11 For so an entrance shall be ministered unto you abundantly into the everlasting kingdom of our Lord and Saviour Jesus Christ.
> 12 Wherefore I will not be negligent to put you always in remembrance of these things, though ye know them, and be established in the present truth.

13 Yea, I think it meet, as long as I am in this tabernacle, to stir you up by putting you in remembrance;
14 Knowing that shortly I must put off this my tabernacle, even as our Lord Jesus Christ hath showed me.

1. **Productiveness (v. 8).**—For the individual believer, the consequences of practicing spiritual addition ("add to your faith," v. 5) begin with fruitful living. Verse 9 presents the alternative in terms of spiritual blindness, inability to recognize and respond to revealed truth.

2. **Confidence (v. 10).**—Faith that is undeveloped can become a wavering faith. On the other hand, making every endeavor to attain spiritual maturity results in increasing enjoyment of salvation's blessings. It is also a protection against stumbling into sin. The active, maturing Christian is less likely to become a victim of Satan's wiles.

3. **Access (v. 11).**—The word translated "add" in verse 5 is repeated here to describe God's action in introducing His people "abundantly into the everlasting kingdom." God will always outdo us in adding, and His overflowing generosity will culminate in bringing us to be with Him forever.

(Our lesson passage concludes with Peter's resolve to keep his readers in constant remembrance of these things that, though known already, cannot be too often repeated. His anticipation of approaching death, which he called putting off "this tabernacle," is related to our Lord's prophetic words in John 21:18-19.)

APPLYING THE LESSON

Some kind words.—Jerome was tired of being on the road. He was assigned a special project by his boss, and consequently, he had to be away from home for ten days in a row. On the tenth day, his discouragement overwhelmed him. As he ordered his food at the restaurant that night, the waitress said, "What do you need?" Jerome responded, "I want some of your lasagna and a few kind words." A few minutes later, the waitress delivered the dish to the table. As she turned to leave, Jerome said, "What about the kind words." The waitress leaned over and whispered in Jerome's ear, "Don't eat the lasagna!"

Sometimes we need words of warning. That was the situation in the early church. In this second epistle, Peter proclaimed a word of warning to the Christians of the first century.

Misplaced focus.—So often we misplace the focus of the Christian life. What does it mean to be a Christian? Simply put, to be a Christian means to believe in Jesus as the Son of God and to commit your life to Him. A man was seeking to lead a young woman to Christ one day. He asked her if she knew the joy of Jesus. Her response was: "No, I can't go to church. I have to work on Sundays." Church is important, but going to church does not make you a

Christian anymore than living in a garage will make you an automobile. From the first century to our century, Christians have had to continually focus on the essence of Christianity: personal faith in and commitment to Jesus Christ.

God's promises are for us.—A woman had an unusual dream. She saw a room crowded with people who were all obviously distraught. Suddenly, the door of the room opened, and Jesus Himself walked in. He moved from person to person. To each one He said, "My child, why are you crying?"

The first one answered, "I'm crying, Lord, because my husband died when we were so young, and from then on I was just lost without Him. I wanted to serve You, but I was too lonely and upset all those years to do anything." Jesus responded, "Didn't you get my letter?" "What letter, Lord?" came the reply. Jesus said, "I wrote you a letter and told you not to worry, that you believed in God, to believe also in me, and that I would not leave you comfortless." The woman looked surprised. "The minister read that letter at my husband's funeral, but I didn't know it was personal, from You to me."

Jesus stepped to the next person in the room. The man said, "Lord, I couldn't live for You because there were too many things I always had to be worrying about." Jesus said, "Did you not get a letter either?" The man responded, "Did You write me a letter?" "Yes," Jesus replied, "In it I told you about the birds of the air. They don't worry about their next meal, and yet they are fed. I told you to put Me first, for I had work for you to do, and I'd give you everything you really needed." The man said, "I remember reading about that, but I didn't know You meant it for me!"

Around the room Jesus went. For every malady He had words of healing and help from Scripture. But no one had taken the words to heart. For Christians of every century, God's provisions through Christ are personal, and they are adequate.

Two contrasting attitudes.—Notice the difference between these two attitudes.

One was the attitude of the father of D. T. Niles, a widely known Christian leader from Ceylon. Niles's father read the Bible through every year to deepen his knowledge of the Christian faith, and he read Shakespeare's writings every year to deepen his knowledge of human nature. This deepening of knowledge led in turn to a deepening of his faith.

The other attitude was the attitude revealed in an advertisement in the paper. The advertisement was for the sale of a set of encyclopedias. The ad was put into the paper by a certain woman who explained why she was selling her encyclopedias: "My husband knows everything."

One of these two attitudes is reflected in the life of every Christian. Some face each day with a hunger and thirst for more knowledge. Others face each day with the assumption they know everything. Peter's challenge to spiritual growth is in tune with the first of those two attitudes.

TEACHING THE LESSON

Main Idea: Growing in Christian qualities is a necessity for protection against spiritual error.

Suggested Teaching Aim: Learners will explain the need for, the meaning of, and the way to grow in Christian qualities.

Introduce the Bible Study

Share information from *Studying the Bible* that will introduce the study in 2 Peter. Share the comments titled "Some kind words" (*Applying the Lesson*). Note that Peter's words of warning are out of consideration for the well-being of his readers.

Write the main idea on the chalkboard. State that this is Peter's warning in the passage for study today. Ask: What does it mean to grow as a Christian? After their response, share the comments titled "Misplaced focus" (*Applying the Lesson*).

A Teaching Outline
1. Introduce the study in 2 Peter.
2. Focus on growing as a Christian.
3. Discover the need for growing, the meaning of growth, and how to grow in Christian qualities.

State that the purpose of the study today is to help us learn ways to grow in Christian qualities that will help protect us from spiritual error. Invite learners to open their Bibles to 2 Peter 1.

Search for Biblical Truth

Display this outline to guide the Bible study.

> Growing in Grace
> 2 Peter 1:1-14
> 1. A believer's privileges (vv. 1-4)
>   a. Knowledge of God
>   b. Adequate provision
>   c. Precious promises
> 2. A believer's responsibilities (vv. 5-7)
> 3. A believer's prospects (vv. 8-14)
>   a. Productiveness
>   b. Confidence
>   c. Access

Call attention to the first section of the outline. Direct learners to study verses 1-4 to find the verse that supports each of the privileges noted in the outline. Write the verse beside the privilege when it is identified (knowledge, v. 2; provisions, v. 3; promises, v. 4a). Share the comments titled "God's promises are for us" (*Applying the Lesson*).

Note that the believer's privileges provide incentive to meet the believer's responsibilities mentioned in verses 5-7. Direct learners to find eight qualities in which Christians are to grow. After a moment of study, list the qualities on the chalkboard. Direct learners to write them down. Ask: What do these qualities look like in our lives? What do the words mean? Direct learners to discuss the words with those sitting near them to determine what they mean and how they would act if they develop that quality. After a period of study, call for conclusions to be shared.

Continue the Bible study by directing learners to read verses 8-14 and match a verse with the believer's prospect indicated on the outline. After a time of study, call for response. Write the verses on the outline (productiveness, v. 8; confidence, v. 10; access, v. 11). Share the comments titled "Two contrasting attitudes" (*Applying the Lesson*).

Give the Truth a Personal Focus

Ask: How can developing the Christian qualities listed here by Peter protect you against spiritual error? As they respond, establish that the need to grow in these Christian virtues is imperative.

Ask: How does a believer develop these characteristics? Encourage learners to commit themselves to those behaviors that will develop these qualities.

May 31

Focused on the Future

Basic Passage: 2 Peter 3:3-14

Focal Passage: 2 Peter 3:3-14

The story of Jesus is without beginning or end. We may think of His life on earth as starting in Bethlehem and ending at Calvary, or on the Mount of Olives where He ascended to His Father. The clear teaching of Scripture is in His eternal existence He shared in the creation of the universe (Col. 1:16-17), now "ever liveth to make intercession" for His people (Heb. 7:25), is coming again for the redeemed (1 Thess. 4:16), and will forever reign after the "kingdom of the world has become the kingdom of our Lord and of his Messiah" (Rev. 11:15, NRSV). The next great event in this divine biography will be His return to earth as He promised (John 14:3) and as angels foretold after His ascension (Acts 1:10-11). The hope of Jesus' return has led to much speculation and many misleading claims, in spite of His plain statement, "But of that day and hour knoweth no man, no, not the angels of heaven, but my Father only" (Matt. 24:36). Our lesson material reproves some false conclusions while it reaffirms the fact of Christ's return and exhorts to appropriate conduct.

Study Aim: *To reexamine our attitude toward our Lord's return both in belief and behavior*

STUDYING THE BIBLE

Chapter 3 opens with reference to "This second epistle," probably meaning 1 Peter, although we must acknowledge that some other document may have existed of which we are unaware. This is a friendly chapter—note the repeated use of "beloved" (vv. 1,8,14,17)—in spite of the reproof it contains, and it ends with a splendid exhortation and doxology (v. 18). May this study enable us to "grow in grace, and in the knowledge of our Lord and Savior Jesus Christ."

I. Christ's Return Repudiated (2 Pet. 3:3-7)

Earlier in this letter, Peter had acknowledged that the things he was writing about were already known to his readers (1:12-13). The same is stated in 3:1 and puts emphasis on the unfortunate fact that knowing and doing are two different things. We have the same thought in James 1:22. In spite of careful teaching, some of Peter's readers were falling into serious error. Head knowledge is not enough. Commitment of heart and will are also necessary.

> 3 Knowing this first, that there shall come in the last days scoffers, walking after their own lusts,
> 4 And saying, Where is the promise of his coming? for since the fathers fell asleep, all things continue as they were from the beginning of the creation.
> 5 For this they willingly are ignorant of, that by the word of God the heavens were of old, and the earth standing out of the water and in the water:
> 6 Whereby the world that then was, being overflowed with water, perished:
> 7 But the heavens and the earth, which are now, by the same word are kept in store, reserved unto fire against the day of judgment and perdition of ungodly men.

1. Scoffers described (vv. 3-4).—Among things that should have been known and remembered was that prophets and apostles spoke of a falling away from the true faith. Illustrative of this was the presence of persons, within the church, who were making ridicule of teaching about the Lord's return. These were saying that history was pursuing its course without any such event. Generations were born and died, and nothing happened; everything continued along a normal course without any divine intervention. Of these particular persons Peter said that they were "walking after their own lusts," that is, living in complete disregard of morality. We must not understand this to mean that persons with independent ideas about the Lord's coming are necessarily evil, only that this was true of those Peter described.

2. God always active (vv. 5-7).—The apostle went back to the Genesis account of creation to remind his readers of the activity of God. At creation God caused the earth to rise out of the waters (Gen. 1:9), but He later permitted the flood when the world was "overflowed with water," a divine act of judgment. At that time, He promised Noah that He would not so destroy the earth again (Gen. 9:11). The next judgment, according to Peter, would be by fire (see also v. 10). According to the latter verse, this fiery judgment would also be accompanied by "a great noise." In these days of nuclear bombs and missiles, it is easy to think of their destructive power. Peter was not saying that the earth's inhabitants would destroy themselves and their environments, but he meant that God would use these means. However we understand Peter's statement, he was describing a fiery end to conditions as they are, with God in control.

II. Christ's Return Affirmed (2 Pet. 3:8-10)

Peter had three other arguments to use against those who, because of the passing of time, doubted Christ's return and accordingly allowed themselves to slip into careless ways. Together they constitute a strong affirmation of the doctrine of the second coming, and they are important to us who, as we anticipate the twenty-first century, need to be reminded of the abiding value of biblical teaching.

> 8 But, beloved, be not ignorant of this one thing, that one day is with the Lord as a thousand years, and a thousand years as one day.
> 9 The Lord is not slack concerning his promise, as some men count slackness; but is long-suffering to us-ward, not willing that any should perish, but that all should come to repentance.
> 10 But the day of the Lord will come as a thief in the night; in the which the heavens shall pass away with a great noise, and the elements shall melt with fervent heat, the earth also and the works that are therein shall be burned up.

1. **Time and timelessness (v. 8).**—We are creatures of time. Our lives are ordered by clocks and calendars. Not so God. One of the hardest things for us to grasp is His eternity, without beginning and without end. One of Israel's psalmists, reaching for this truth, described God as "from everlasting to everlasting," and said of Him, "For a thousand years in thy sight are but as yesterday when it is past, and as a watch in the night" (Ps. 90:2,4). Peter reproduced this thought in order to help his readers understand that the activity of God cannot be measured by any human standard of time. We reckon the incidents of our Lord's life as taking place two thousand years ago. But if God were subject to any form of chronology, which He is not, this could be no more than two days ago. Even to make this statement is to attempt the impossible, for we are at a loss to comprehend God's eternal existence. It belongs to the mystery of Deity.

2. **Compassionate delay (v. 9).**—More readily understood is the apostle's statement that, if we think in terms of a delayed return of our Lord, we should regard this as evidence of God's compassion for sinners. In Old Testament times, persons who lived in expectation of a coming "day of the Lord" were warned that it would come as a day of

judgment, "darkness, and not light" (Amos 5:18). Likewise the coming again of the Lord Jesus is described in a dual light, gain immeasurable for His people, and loss indescribable for the disobedient and unbelieving (Matt. 24:29-31). So long as Jesus does not come, opportunity is present for persons to repent and believe. During this period, it behooves God's people to be messengers of His gospel that all may hear and exercise faith, and so become part of the redeemed.

[margin note: we must present the gospel to the lost]

3. Sudden and unexpected (v. 10).—Our writer's emphasis is strong and powerful, "But the day of the Lord will come." Let doubters beware and the indifferent arouse themselves, for God's purposes are sure. Moreover, that day will come without warning and so catch many by surprise. Jesus had used the analogy of a thief when speaking of His return, and the apostle Paul echoed the idea when he wrote, "the day of the Lord so cometh as a thief in the night" (1 Thess. 5:2). The focus is on the unexpectedness of a thief's action. He does not announce his coming in advance but takes his victims by surprise. Yet people continue to fix dates for the second coming and add their names to a long list of false prophets who claim to know what Jesus Himself made no claim to knowing (Matt. 24:36).

[margin note: No one knows the time of His return except GOD]

III. Christ's Return Motivating (2 Pet. 3:11-14)

Our Lord gave several parables related to the need for active watchfulness on the part of those who look for His coming again. Three are grouped in Matthew 24:42—25:30. This is the theme of the following verses from 2 Peter:

> 11 Seeing then that all these things shall be dissolved, what manner of persons ought ye to be in all holy conversation and godliness,
> 12 Looking for and hasting unto the coming of the day of God, wherein the heavens being on fire shall be dissolved, and the elements shall melt with fervent heat?
> 13 Nevertheless we, according to his promise, look for new heavens and a new earth, wherein dwelleth righteousness.
> 14 Wherefore, beloved, seeing that ye look for such things, be diligent that ye may be found of him in peace, without spot, and blameless.

1. Expectant living (vv. 11-12).—The knowledge that our Lord may be revealed in power at any moment should have a sobering effect on His people. Are there places where we would not wish Him to find us? Activities that we would not wish Him to see? An old spiritual says, "He'll find me hoeing cotton when He comes," that is, busy about my rightful tasks and therefore unashamed to face Him. In verse 11, "conversation," as elsewhere in the *King James Version*, means "manner of life," and that, of course, includes speech, its character and content.

2. **A new beginning (vv. 13-14).**—In line with the Book of Revelation, this epistle looks into the future and sees "a new heaven and a new earth: for the first heaven and the first earth were passed away" (Rev. 21:1). The destruction earlier described precedes a new beginning and a cosmos "wherein dwelleth righteousness." Peter did not elaborate on this glorious prospect, but had he done so, it would surely have been in terms similar to Revelation 21:1-8 and 22:1-5. God has plans for a new creation, in which all His redeemed people will share in the joys. Meanwhile, He waits in order that the number of the redeemed may be multiplied.

APPLYING THE LESSON

Till Jesus comes.—The prediction of Jesus' return permeates the New Testament. Because of the certainty of His coming, we need to be ready. BO Baker in *The Lift of Love* makes some pertinent suggestions, here quoted, on what to do until Jesus comes:

1. Be sure that your salvation is firmly grounded in the person of Jesus Christ.
2. Deal thoroughly with any and all unconfessed sin and spiritual unfaithfulness. . . .
3. Deposit daily some acts of Christian love and service in heaven. . . .
4. Do today what the Holy Spirit impresses you to do without delay or the slightest anticipation that someone else will do it for you.
5. Feed upon the Word of God in order that you may have some understanding of the place, the plan, and the people with whom you will spend eternity.
6. Live your faith as a natural experience and not as an unnatural phenomenon.
7. Cultivate a consistent prayer life which forbids a fear of the unknown.
8. Make a serious and honest effort to so witness to the saving grace of God that others like you will be ready to meet Jesus when He comes.[1]

Prayer in a wagon.—A man who lived in the country fell and broke his leg. He was confined to his house for a long period of time. He had a large family and thus needed some help. The Christian friends at church held a prayer meeting to pray for this family. While the people were praying and asking God to help the family, there was a loud knock on the door of this needy family's home. A young boy stood at the door. He said to the needy family, "My father could not attend the prayer meeting tonight, so he just sent his prayers in a wagon." On this wagon were potatoes, meat, apples, and other things to help the needy family. Prayer is important, but allowing us to be instruments by which our prayers are fulfilled is even more important. In the

Christian life, what's most important is not what we know to do or what we want to do but what we actually do.

Today.—As creatures of time, we are aware of our past and anticipatory about our future, but the time in which we must live is *today*. Yesterday is a canceled check. Tomorrow is a promissory note. Only today is currency we can spend. Someone made three suggestions about today: today is all you have, today is all you can manage, and today is all you need. Each of those statements is true about us. The Bible says we have a God who is not limited by today, who is not confined by today, nor is He exhausted by today. He is God for whom "one day is . . . as a thousand years, and a thousand years as one day" (2 Pet. 3:8). *Patience*

The queen of virtues.—Do you know what Chrysostom, the golden-tongued orator of another generation, called the "queen of virtues"? He was referring to patience.

Charles Allen, a gifted communicator of our generation, addressed the subject from the other direction. He said that the worse sin in America is staying too busy, as if by our busy-ness we can rush things according to our plans.

Most of us come closer to committing the sin of "busy-ness" than in exhibiting the virtue of "patience." Patience, like all virtues, is displayed in its perfect form in God. God's patience is rooted in His compassion for humankind and His desire that humankind will hear and heed His word.

Motivation for a productive life.—Many things motivate us to be our best. Martin Niemoeller, German patriot who opposed Hitler, said that whenever he was tempted to give up, he was motivated by a vision of the German youth of the future. Sam Rayburn, famous politician, was motivated by a challenge given to him as a young man by his father who said, "Sam, be a man." Larry Bird, one of the greatest professional basketball players of today, admits that much of his motivation came from those who doubted his ability. He wanted to prove them wrong.

The greatest motivation for the Christian is the fact that someday Jesus Christ will return, and we will have to give an account of our lives to Him. How wonderful it would be to hear Him say to us, "Well done, good and faithful servant."

TEACHING THE CLASS

Main Idea: The return of Jesus Christ is a fact that must affect how we live our lives.

Suggested Teaching Aim: Learners will evaluate their beliefs and their behavior related to the return of Jesus Christ.

Introduce the Bible Study

Share the comments titled "Motivation for a productive life" (*Applying the Lesson*). Note that this final study in 2 Peter emphasizes the return of Jesus Christ.

Ask: What do you know about the second coming of Christ? Elicit response. Encourage learners to express their thoughts even if unsure of the facts. Point out that while there may be disagreement about the sequence of events related to the return of Christ, the fact of His return is clearly taught in the Scripture.

Ask: What is the purpose of knowing that Jesus will return to earth again? What difference does that make? Responses may include the hope that the fact gives and confidence in their faith. If it is not included, point out that the fact of His return should also make a difference in the way we live our lives until His return.

State that the purpose of the study today is to help us evaluate both our beliefs about the return of Christ and our behavior in view of the fact of His return. Invite learners to open their Bibles to 2 Peter 3.

Search for Biblical Truth

Use information from *Studying the Bible* to provide background for this Scripture passage. State that in the day in which Peter wrote there were those who scoffed at the idea that Jesus would return to earth. Direct learners to read verses 3-4 to themselves to learn what the scoffers were saying. Call for response. (Everything is as it always has been. Nothing will change.)

A Teaching Outline
1. Focus on the return of Jesus.
2. Discover some facts about His return that were emphasized by Peter.
3. Evaluate personal beliefs and behavior in view of these facts.
4. Decide to pursue more appropriate behavior in view of the sure return of Jesus.

Note that Peter refuted their statement in verses 5-7. Call on a learner to read the verses aloud. Note that Peter affirmed that God is always at work. Use information from *Studying the Bible* to supplement comments.

State that Peter gave explanation of why it seems that nothing will change to the scoffer in verse 8. Call on a learner to read the verse aloud. Note that it is a commonly quoted verse. Ask learners to read verse 9 to themselves and discover the reason why God delays Jesus' coming. Call for response. Share the comments titled "The queen of virtues" (*Applying the Lesson*).

State that verse 10 begins Peter's description of the return of the Lord. Call on a learner to read the verse aloud. Compare this information with other information provided by learners as the study was begun.

Share that Peter now began to give instruction about how believers ought to respond in view of the sure return of Christ. Direct learners to read verses 11-14 silently. When the reading is finished, direct learners to work with those sitting near them to develop a list of Peter's instructions for living in view of the return of Jesus. After several minutes, invite learners to share their conclusions.

Give the Truth a Personal Focus

Share the information from *Applying the Lesson* titled "Till Jesus comes." If possible, provide learners copies of the points suggesting that these are very practical ways to live out the instructions of Peter.

Conclude the unit of study by asking learners to share their impressions of the writings of Peter, what his primary emphasis seems to be, and how it has influenced their thinking and behavior.

---

1. BO Baker, *The Lift of Love* (Nashville: Broadman Press, 1986), 122-23.

June, July, August 1992

God's Judgment and Mercy

Aids from BROADMAN for Studying and Teaching

Books:
The Broadman Bible Commentary, Volume 7
Layman's Bible Book Commentary, Volumes 13,14
Strong's Exhaustive Concordance, James Strong
The Heart of Hebrew History, H. I. Hester

Apart from a few of the Minor Prophets such as Hosea, Amos, and Jonah, these ancient pronouncements seldom find their way into Sunday School curriculum. In this series we are to make acquaintance with some of the lesser-known books that conclude the Old Testament: Obadiah, Nahum, and Zephaniah among them. There are two units of lessons, as follows:

Unit I, "Warnings and Promises from God," deals with prophecies of judgment against the people of Israel and other nations. God's universal sovereignty will be brought into sharp focus.

June 7

The Lord Will Restore Judah

Basic Passage: Obadiah

Focal Passages: Obadiah 1-4,10-11,15,17,21

Unfamiliar passages of Scripture are always a challenge. The little prophecy of Obadiah, only twenty-one verses, is probably among the least known of the books of the Bible. A strong note of condemnation prevails throughout the book as the prophet denounced the people of Edom for their treachery against Israel and pronounced their doom. The one positive note is the sovereignty of God who is active in history to bring deliverance to His people. A New Testament parallel may be found in recent lessons on Peter's Epistles in which the persecuted church was assured of judgment on its enemies and an abundant entrance "into the everlasting kingdom of our Lord and Savior Jesus Christ" (2 Pet. 1:11). Old Testament prophecies of a restored Israel were fulfilled in the return from Babylonian captivity and the rebuilding of Jerusalem. Our anticipation is not an earthly kingdom but a heavenly, again to quote Peter, "wherein dwelleth righteousness" (2 Pet. 3:13).

Study Aim: *To recognize God at work in history and trust His promises for the future*

STUDYING THE BIBLE

Edomites were descendants of Esau. The hostility evidenced at the birth of the twins, Jacob and Esau (Gen. 25:21-23), continued through many centuries. The Edomites, who occupied territory south of the Dead Sea, refused the plea of Moses to be allowed to lead the Israelites through their territory and threatened violence if they attempted this (Num. 20:14-21). Consequently, "Edom and Israel scorned and hated each other throughout their whole history. For centuries there existed between them an implacable animosity. They constantly waged a war of revenge against each other."[1] There were clashes between the two during Saul's reign, but David subdued the Edomites (2 Sam. 8:14). In later years, they repeatedly rebelled; and in Jehoram's reign, they revolted, selected a king, and attacked Judah (2 Chron. 21:8-10). This is the background against which Obadiah's prophecy must be studied.

I. Pride Leads to a Fall (Obad. 1-4)

Obadiah is among the common names of the Old Testament; and in the absence of information about the author in the book that bears this name, we are not able to identify him. Neither can any final determination be made as to the date of writing, but see comments below on verses 10-14.

> 1 The vision of Obadiah. Thus saith the Lord concerning Edom; We have heard a rumor from the Lord, and an ambassador is sent among the heathen, Arise, ye, and let us rise up against her in battle.
> 2 Behold, I have made thee small among the heathen: thou art greatly despised.
> 3 The pride of thine heart hath deceived thee, thou that dwellest in the clefts of the rock, whose habitation is high; that saith in his heart, Who shall bring me down to the ground?
> 4 Though thou exalt thyself as the eagle, and though thou set thy nest among the stars, thence will I bring thee down, saith the Lord.

1. Call to arms (v. 1).—Our understanding is helped by this translation, "We have heard a report from the Lord, / and a messenger has been sent among the nations" (NRSV). "Nations" should also be read for "heathen" in verse 2. A call to arms against Edom is issued, in God's name, to surrounding nations. People who had been acting in arrogance against others were due for a fall. Though big and important in their own estimation, they would be reduced to insignificance and accordingly despised by others.

2. False confidence (vv. 2-4).—The pride of the Edomites was expressed in the towering rocks in which they lived. Modern tourists in the Middle East are still fascinated by the rock city of Petra, successor to the Edomite stronghold. Most Bible dictionaries contain pictures of impressive structures hewn out of solid stone. These structures were the work of an Arab people known as Nabateans who drove out the Edomites somewhere around 300 B.C. Edomite ruins have been found in the area. The physical appearance of Petra and its neighborhood fits well into the description given in verses 3-4 as the territory occupied by Edom.

II. Callous Indifference Rebuked (Obad. 10-14)

Verses 5-9 anticipate the coming destruction of Edom. Their enemy would not be like a common thief who would take what he wanted and spare the rest, or a gatherer of grapes who would take all he needed and no more. Those upon whom the Edomites had relied for help would forsake them. The reference to "wise men" (v. 8) acknowledges that among these people were those highly rated as scholars. Neither mountain strongholds nor brains would suffice in the coming day of judgment. In two places in this passage, "Esau" is used for Edom. Teman (v. 9) was an Edomite city.

> 10 For thy violence against thy brother Jacob shame shall cover thee, and thou shalt be cut off forever.
> 11 In the day that thou stoodest on the other side, in the day that the strangers carried away captive his forces, and foreigners entered into his gates, and cast lots upon Jerusalem, even thou wast as one of them.

1. Aiding Israel's enemies (vv. 10-11).—By ancestry, Edomites were descended from Esau and Israelites from Jacob, hence the use of "Jacob" (v. 10). The charge made is that the Edomites took "the other side" by aiding the enemies of Jerusalem when they attacked that city. The precise occasion is not given, but the consensus of opinion favors the Babylonian assault (587 B.C.) when the city was destroyed and its people taken into exile.

2. Detailed accusations (vv. 12-14).—The Edomites did not merely stand aside in Jerusalem's hour of need, but they actively supported the Babylonians. They actually entered the city, gloated (NRSV) over the disaster that had befallen it, joined the enemy in looting its contents, cut off the escape of fleeing citizens, and delivered them into the hands of the attackers. The phrase, "You should not," (NRSV) introduces eight distinct charges made against Edom for which God would call them to account.

III. Divine Justice at Work (Obad. 15-16)

The prophetic word against Edom was, "As thou hast done, it shall be done unto thee" (v. 15). A century or more after the fall of Jerusalem, Nabatean Arabs forced the Edomites out of the rocky fortresses that are now Petra and drove them south into an area that became known as Idumea. Later, in the period of the Maccabees, they were forcibly incorporated into the Jewish community with which, of course, they already had a blood relationship. The Herods were Idumeans. When Rome subdued and destroyed Jerusalem in A.D. 70, Edomites fought alongside the inhabitants of the city. A secular source, however, accuses them of treachery. Whether or not, from this point on they disappeared as a recognizable people from the pages of history.

> 15 For the day of the Lord is near upon all the heathen: as thou hast done, it shall be done unto thee: thy reward shall return upon thine own head.

The emphasis is on the judgments and sovereignty of God. Edom had boasted, "Who shall bring me down to the ground?" (v. 3), and the answer was, "Thence will I bring thee down, saith the Lord" (v. 4). Verse 16 goes beyond the fate of Edom and declares that "all the nations around you" (NRSV) will similarly fall if they resist the purposes of the Lord. In this verse, references to drinking do not refer to refreshment but to judgment; violators will drink of the cup of divine wrath. Of Edom it became true, "They shall be as though they had not been." A casual knowledge of history can produce other names of nations, small and great, that have disappeared: Babylon, for example; Assyria; the Greek and Roman empires, mighty in their day, oppressive in their policies, and now no more. Even the Northern Kingdom of Israel, after the destruction of Samaria its capital, passed into oblivion, its people apparently being merged into the general Jewish population of Palestine. There are modern examples, also, so that the warning is clear to all nations who oppose the purposes of and despise God's laws.

IV. God's Care for His People (Obad. 17-21)

The vision of God's prophets extended far beyond current events, or those in the near future. Their messages related to these, as when Obadiah foretold the fate of Edom. But in his concluding verse, this prophet reached into the distant future when the reign of God would prevail.

> 17 But upon mount Zion shall be deliverance, and there shall be holiness; and the house of Jacob shall possess their possessions.
> ....
> 21 And saviors shall come up on mount Zion to judge the mount of Esau; and the kingdom shall be the Lord's.

1. Jerusalem's security (v. 17).—Under the name of mount Zion, Jerusalem is promised deliverance from its enemies. We do not know when Obadiah's words were written, but they appear to refer to the return from exile when the walls of the city were rebuilt and the temple restored. The statement "There shall be holiness" can be variously understood. It can mean that Jerusalem would again be a sacred place and, therefore, under the protection of the Lord. Moreover, "the house of Jacob"—the Israelites as a whole—would recover lost possessions, probably lands occupied during the exile.

2. Possessions recovered (vv. 18-20).—The "house of Jacob" mentioned together with "the house of Joseph" (v. 18) indicated a coming together of the two kingdoms of Judah and Israel. The times of the divided kingdom would end. Together they would execute judgment on "the house of Esau" (Edom). Other neighboring people also took advantage of Israel's misfortunes. They too would be dispossessed of land that was not theirs by right (vv. 19-20).

3. Justice enthroned (v. 21).—All this spoke of the ultimate victory of God over His foes and the foes of His people. Looking into the distant future, the prophet wrote, "The kingdom shall be the Lord's." This note of optimistic expectations is characteristic of all Israel's prophets. No matter how dark a picture they presented, the prophets invariably concluded with a triumphant message that declared God to be in charge of history, of which He would write the ultimate chapter. Though nations rise and fall, His kingdom stands firm and will be revealed one day in all its splendor.

APPLYING THE LESSON

Sowing and reaping.—William McKinley, who later became president of the United States, was on a streetcar one night. He took the last empty seat at the rear of the car. At one of the stops, an old washer woman, carrying a heavy basket, boarded the car. With no place to sit, she stood in the aisle. A man was sitting right in front of the old lady, but he shifted his newspaper in such a way as to act like he didn't see her. McKinley walked down the aisle, picked up the basket of washing, and led the old lady back to his seat.

What seemed to be nothing more than a slight unkindness by the man who refused to help was in fact more than that. This man who displayed obvious unconcern was a politician who held public office. Many years later, McKinley was trying to decide between two men to appoint to an important diplomatic post. Suddenly, McKinley remembered the incident from the streetcar many years earlier, for the man who had refused to offer a seat to the lady was one of the candidates for the diplomatic seat. McKinley gave the position to the other candidate. The man never knew that his act of unkindness would later deprive him of what would have been the most important opportunity in his life.

This story illustrates a truth that is at the heart of the Book of Obadiah: what we sow we will eventually reap.

Watch out for your enemies.—Yogi Berra became a famous baseball player not only because of his ability but also because of some of the "tricks of the trade" that he learned over the years. For example, Ken Harrelson, who later became a great baseball player himself, came to the plate for his first time at bat in the big leagues. It was Yankee Stadium, NBC game of the week. Whitey Ford was pitching. Yogi Berra was catching. The first pitch was a strike. The second pitch was a strike. With two strikes, Harrelson tensed up. His mother was watching him play on television, and he did not want to strike out. Just before the next pitch came, Harrelson said, he felt something warm on the back of his sock. He glanced down to see what it was as the pitch swished by for strike three. Yogi had spit on the back of his leg to distract him, and while he was distracted, Whitey Ford zipped in the third strike. Harrelson was dumbfounded. Yogi grinned and said, "Welcome to the big leagues, kid!"

"All's fair in love and war" is an adage that applies to professional baseball. Unfortunately, we also apply that adage to our relationships with other people. Consequently, we do things to our enemies that we would not do in normal circumstances. That truth explains the intensity of feelings between the Israelites and the Edomites. The hatred of these two nations for each other, which was rooted in their earliest history, was reflected in the unkind actions and attitudes they manifested toward each other.

Two sides of pride.—Pride is condemned in the Bible and from the pulpit, but the word *pride* has two sides. Pride can be commendable when it expresses a healthy sense of contentment with who we are and what we have accomplished. Such pride is expressed in Paul's familiar statement, "I can do all things through Him who strengthens me" (Phil. 4:13, NASB). However, pride has another face. Pride can also be defined as "an excessively high opinion of oneself." This kind of pride can be called "conceit," and it is condemned unequivocally in the Bible. This second kind of pride characterized the Edomites.

Typo or the truth?—Sometimes typographical errors reveal more truth about us than we like. One rather cold, sophisticated church wanted to create an air of compassion and concern. So at the bottom of the bulletin each Sunday, they printed this statement, "We take interest in everyone." However, one week a typographical error produced another revealing version. The typo said, "We fake interest in everyone."

The Edomites did not even "fake" interest in the Israelites. Theirs was an obvious and intense dislike, and this feeling was revealed in their gloating over the defeat of Israel.

TEACHING THE CLASS

Main Idea: God's righteous indignation can bring human downfall.
Suggested Teaching Aim: Learners will describe the quality of God that reflects indignance and consider righteous indignation in their lives.

Introduce the Bible Study

Write *Obadiah, Nahum, Zephaniah, Jonah* on the chalkboard. Direct learners to locate the books in their Bibles. Use information from the introduction to the study for the quarter to comment about the two units from these books. Write the names of the units on the chalkboard.

A Teaching Outline
1. Introduce the study, "God's Judgment and Mercy."
2. Introduce the Book of Obadiah and today's study.
3. Discover why God expressed indignation through Obadiah's words.
4. Consider the place of indignation in the response of a believer.
5. Consider the possibility of personal arrogance that brings the indignation of God on learners.

Direct learners to turn again to Obadiah. State that the purpose of today's study is to learn of the righteous indignation of God and its result.

Search for Biblical Truth

Share information from the introduction (*Studying the Bible*) to provide background for understanding the passage. Display the following outline to guide the Bible study.

> Obadiah 1-4,10-11,15,17,21
> I. Pride leads to a fall (vv. 1-4)
> II. Callous indifference rebuked (vv. 10-14)
> III. Divine justice at work (vv. 15-16)
> IV. God's care for His people (vv. 17-21)

Call on a learner to read verses 1-4 aloud after noting the outline heading for these verses. Use information from *Studying the Bible* to comment about Edom's false confidence.

Share the comments titled "Sowing and reaping"(*Applying the Lesson*). Note that the next section of Scripture for study begins the reaping. Call on a learner to read verses 10 and 11 aloud. Ask: What was the accusation against the Edomites? (They sided with the aggressors against God's people.)

Note that specific accusations are aimed at the Edomites in verses 12-14. Use information from *Studying the Bible* about these verses.

Call attention to the third heading. Call on a learner to read verse 15 aloud while other learners listen to learn the judgment pronounced. Call for response.

Note the future focus of the next verses. Call attention to the outline heading. Use information from *Studying the Bible* to clarify the meaning. Call on a learner to read verses 17 and 21 aloud.

Give the Truth a Personal Focus

Share the story titled "Typo or the truth?" (*Applying the Lesson*). Note that such arrogant behavior caused God to look on the Edomites with condemnation. Their pride created indignation in the response of God. Share the comments about pride found in the paragraph titled "Two sides of pride" (*Applying the Lesson*).

Ask rhetorically: Is God justified in expressing indignation at behavior like that of the Edomites? Continue: Are Christians ever justified in expressing indignation about the behavior of other people? If so, when and in what circumstances? Elicit response. Discuss appropriate ways of expressing indignation.

Continue by asking rhetorically: Are there behaviors and attitudes about which God might be indignant in our own lives? Do you have some of the arrogant characteristics of the Edomites? How would God deal with you in such circumstances? Allow several minutes for learners to consider their own relationship with God.

---

1. George L. Robinson, *The Twelve Minor Prophets* (Grand Rapids: Baker Book House, 1952), 67.

June 14

Fleeing From God

Basic Passage: Jonah 1—2

Focal Passages: Jonah 1:1-9,15-17

Racial prejudice is not new. In our previous lesson we saw how enmity existed, for long centuries, between Israel and Edom. Explanations for this are not difficult to find. But the fact remains that these two contestants were descended from twin brothers, Jacob and Esau, and should have learned how to live in peace with one another. There were no close blood ties between Israel and Assyria, a nation that terrorized its neighbors until its eclipse around 612 B.C. For Jonah to be sent by God as missionary to Nineveh, capital of Assyria, meant ministering to his nation's worst enemy. He was not prepared to do that and went to great lengths to escape the responsibility given to him. His story is left open-ended, with no conclusive finish. Jonah was left sitting on a bluff, waiting to "see what would become of the city" (4:5). He knew well his God-given duty but still struggled with his prejudices. Isn't this the condition of many people today in a world divided by hatred and mistrust?

Study Aim: *To face our prejudices, identify them, and resolve what we should do with them in light of the teaching of Christ*

STUDYING THE BIBLE

The Book of Jonah falls into four dramatic scenes, conveniently marked by its four chapters. It bears Jonah's name but was written by some other anonymous person, with the exception of the prayer in chapter 2. When it was written is difficult to determine, but its message suits a time, possibly after the Babylonian exile, when the Jewish people were expressing a high sense of national pride with a corresponding disdain for other nations.

I. The Man and His Book

Critical scholarship has tried to present the Book of Jonah as an allegory, with no historical basis. This ignores clear statements about the prophet, in both the Old and New Testaments. In our attempts to interpret the book we should remember that it was written after (perhaps long after) the events described. The author found in Jonah's story a much-needed message for his own times.

1. Jonah's period.—The Old Testament reference to Jonah is in 2 Kings 14:23-27 where he is said to have foretold the victories of Jeroboam II, king of Israel. His identity is confirmed by his being described as the son of Amittai (see Jonah 1:1). In spite of Jeroboam's evil reign, this was a time of national recovery for the Northern Kingdom. We may assume that Jonah was happy as messenger of good tidings to the king's court and had no desire to change his job. Our Lord compared Jonah's adventure in the big fish with His own burial and resurrection (Matt. 12:38-42; 16:4). His reference was coupled with another to the "queen of the south," that is, Sheba (12:42), an unquestioned historical figure.

2. The book's purpose.—There were other prophets to Israel around Jonah's time, namely, Amos and Hosea. Unlike Jonah, these men reproved national sin with a strong emphasis on social oppression. So we have a picture of a nation "externally strong, prosperous, and confident of the future" but "inwardly rotten and sick past curing."[1] Material prosperity and military success blinded the people to their true condition and encouraged a national pride that was their undoing. The archenemy, Assyria, was in decline, and this encouraged a sense of superiority that expressed itself in a distorted patriotism. These dangerous attitudes were to be repeated in later history, so Jonah's story was revived in order to rebuke and correct a spirit that had brought previous disaster. God's universal compassion was an idea that had been buried by a deluge of pride and prejudice.

II. Jonah's Commission (Jonah 1:1-3)

The court prophet's easygoing life was disturbed by an order from God to go preach in Nineveh, Assyria's capital. This was a very ancient city (Gen. 10:11) and, according to all reports, had become one of the more corrupt communities of the ancient East. Jonah, who seems to have closed his eyes to the evil that was going on in Israel, was being sent to a notoriously wicked city whose rulers had long been oppressors of his people.

> 1 Now the word of the Lord came unto Jonah the son of Amittai, saying,
> 2 Arise, go to Nineveh, that great city, and cry against it; for their wickedness is come up before me.
> 3 But Jonah rose up to flee unto Tarshish from the presence of the Lord, and went down to Joppa; and he found a ship going to Tarshish: so he paid the fare thereof and went down into it, to go with them unto Tarshish from the presence of the Lord.

In willful disobedience toward God, Jonah decided to get as far from Nineveh as possible. He was willing to take a long, hard sea voyage to avoid carrying out the divine command. Tarshish is usually located in Spain; and if this was Jonah's destination, it was at the ends of the earth according to the limited geographical knowledge of those days. The Scripture states twice that his flight was "from the presence of the Lord." Does this reveal a misunderstanding of the nature of God? The psalmist asked, "Whither shall I go from thy spirit? or whither shall I flee from thy presence?" (Ps. 139:7). He made several suggestions only to acknowledge that there is no escaping God. This Jonah learned the hard way.

III. Flight and Its Consequences (Jonah 1:4-10)

Important to note are the opening words of verse 4, "But the Lord sent out a great wind." Similar statements are, "Now the Lord had prepared a great fish" (v. 17); "The Lord spake unto the fish" (2:10); "The Lord God prepared a gourd" (4:6); and, "But God prepared a worm" (4:7). We are not dealing with natural processes but with the activity of God in behalf of Jonah, for his instruction, and for instruction of all who read his story.

> 4 But the Lord sent out a great wind into the sea, and there was a mighty tempest in the sea, so that the ship was like to be broken.
> 5 Then the mariners were afraid, and cried every man unto his god, and cast forth the wares that were in the ship into the sea, to lighten it of them. But Jonah was gone down into the sides of the ship; and he lay, and was fast asleep.
> 6 So the shipmaster came to him, and said unto him, What meanest thou, O sleeper? arise, call upon thy God, if so be that God will think upon us, that we perish not.
> 7 And they said everyone to his fellow, Come, and let us cast lots, that we may know for whose cause this evil is upon us. So they cast lots, and the lot fell upon Jonah.
> 8 Then said they unto him, Tell us, we pray thee, for whose cause this evil is upon us; What is thine occupation? and whence comest thou? what is thy country? and of what people art thou?
> 9 And he said unto them, I am an Hebrew; and I fear the Lord, the God of heaven, which hath made the sea and the dry land.

1. Asleep in a storm (vv. 4-6).—This extraordinary storm had the crew, probably Phoenicians, scared to death. Its fury is suggested by the rendering, "But the Lord hurled a great wind" (NRSV). The seamen cried to their gods for help, and then they took practical measures to save themselves by throwing overboard everything that was not nailed down. This was a normal procedure for the purpose of lightening the ship so that it would ride higher in the rough water (see Acts 27:38). Meanwhile, Jonah was fast asleep (the Greek version of the Old Testament reads, "was asleep, and snored"). This must have been a sleep of emotional and physical exhaustion from which the ship's captain had difficulty awakening him. Here was a passenger who was not contributing to the emergency by praying for deliverance, as the crew had done.

2. Confession made (vv. 7-10).—The belief of the pagan seamen was that someone on board was responsible for this furious storm. To find out who, they cast lots, perhaps with stones, perhaps with long and short straws. This procedure pointed to Jonah as the culprit, and he was plied with questions to find out more about him and to possibly obtain explanation for what was happening. In doing this, the crew showed some hesitation in jumping to a conclusion, merely on the basis of the lot. They were giving Jonah a fair chance. In making reply, this reticent prophet did some preaching to the men who shared his danger (v. 9) and then made a surprising confession: he was running away from the Creator God whom he professed to worship ("fear").

IV. A Refuge Provided (Jonah 1:11-17)

Jonah's action in this acute situation shows that he was more of a misguided patriot than a coward. He would not go to Nineveh because its inhabitants were the enemies of his people. But, after being identified as the cause of the storm, he asked to be thrown into the sea that the rest might be saved.

> 15 So they took up Jonah, and cast him forth into the sea: and the sea ceased from her raging.
> 16 Then the men feared the Lord exceedingly, and offered a sacrifice unto the Lord, and made vows.
> 17 Now the Lord had prepared a great fish to swallow up Jonah. And Jonah was in the belly of the fish three days and three nights.

1. Reaction of seamen (vv. 13,14,16).—The efforts of the pagan crew to save Jonah were recorded to their credit. They first tried to row to shore. Then they prayed to Jonah's God and offered a sacrifice to Him. They became examples of the fact that the most unlikely people (Ninevites among them) are capable of responding to the true God.

2. The great fish (v. 17).—This was not necessarily a whale but a specially prepared sea creature, capable of providing a safe refuge for Jonah until lessons had been learned.

V. Prayer from the Depths (Jonah 2)

Our larger lesson includes this chapter. Above all, it illustrates the power of prayer, in this case offered in an unlikely place and by an undeserving person. Jonah acknowledged that what had happened to him was God's judgment (v. 3). In his plight, he made heavy use of the psalms, a reminder of the value of committing God's Word to memory. We never know when we may need its comfort and strength. In confidence of deliverance from his underwater prison, Jonah renewed his earlier vows, and he was cast forth "upon the dry land" (v. 10).

APPLYING THE LESSON

No prejudice.—General Chuck Yeager was a pioneer in aviation history. He was not only the first man to fly faster than the speed of sound, he has also been one of the best test pilots in American history. Accusations of racial prejudice in the air force incensed Yeager. He said, "Nowadays, it has become fashionable for some companies to advertise themselves as 'equal opportunity employers.' The Air Force practiced that with me right from the start, and I would never deny to anybody else the chance to prove his worth, no matter who or what he is. There never were black pilots or white pilots in the Air Force. There were only pilots who knew how to fly, and pilots who didn't."[2]

Yeager may claim an absence of prejudice in the air force. However, the truth is, each of us is often held captive by our prejudices. Our lesson reminds us that this has been a problem for a long time.

God's love revealed.—A play entitled *The Sign of Jonah,* written shortly after World War II, clearly depicts God's love. The setting of the play is Germany right after World War II. The point of the play is to attempt to discover who was to blame for the awful atrocities of the war. One man suggested Hitler was to blame. Another blamed the problems on the Jews. Others declared the real culprit was the apathetic "average person" who did nothing to resist the movement of Hitler. Finally, one man said, "I know whose fault it is. God is to blame. He is the one who made it happen." The crowd agreed, and they decided to take God to court. He was found guilty of the crime of creation, and the judge pronounced the sentence. For punishment of the crime of creation, God was going to have to come and live in the world like human beings do. Three archangels, Gabriel, Michael, and Raphael, were sent to execute the judgment. Gabriel mused to himself, "When God serves this sentence, I'll make sure he knows obscurity and shame. He'll be born in obscurity and will know what it is like to live in an occupied country and be the object of scorn." Then Michael mused to himself, "When God serves His sentence, I'm going to see to it that He knows frustration and insecurity. He'll have no place to lay His head. His family will desert Him. In the end, even His friends will desert Him." Raphael mused to himself, "When God serves this sentence, I'm going to see to it that He knows what it is like to suffer and to die. He will be falsely accused, illegally tried, and will then die the long slow death of a common criminal." At that point, the lights go out, and the play is over. And suddenly the truth becomes clear—God has already served that sentence. He already knows what it's like to live as a human being in this kind of world. He revealed in the incarnation His unconquerable love for the world. The Book of Jonah describes the process by which the prophet came to understand about God's love.

The power of prayer.—You've probably heard the old saying: "Nothing lies beyond the reach of prayer except that which lies outside the will of God." Nowhere is that truth illustrated more clearly than in the experience of Jonah. The Bible is filled with illustrations of those who cried out to God in their time of need and found Him sufficient. However, the danger in these examples is the tendency to think of prayer only in emergency terms.

One little boy was asked by his mother if he had said his prayers before going to bed. "No," the little boy replied, "I didn't need anything."

Another child said to her family, "Does anyone need anything? I'm getting ready to pray."

Yet another child said, "God, My sister is still not married, my mother is still sick, I still failed my history test, and my daddy still doesn't have a job. I'm tired of praying and not getting any results."

When Jonah prayed, he did get results. However, that was not the most important factor about his prayer. The most important thing about Jonah's prayer was that it put him back in touch with God. A richer relationship and not necessarily rich results is the greatest product of prayer.

TEACHING THE CLASS

Main Idea: Prejudice can separate us from God.
Suggested Teaching Aim: Learners will resolve to deal with their own prejudices.

Introduce the Bible Study

Note that the study for today is from Jonah, a book more familiar to most than Obadiah. Ask: As you recall Jonah's story, what would you say were his main problems? Elicit response. Note on chalkboard. If prejudice is not listed, suggest it to learners.

Share the comments from paragraphs titled "No prejudice" (*Applying the Lesson*). Ask: Do you recognize prejudice in yourself? What prejudices do we often have whether we are aware of them or not?

Continue by asking: What is the effect of such prejudices on our relationship with God and on His will being carried out in our lives?

A Teaching Outline
1. Focus on kinds and effects of prejudice.
2. Discover the results of prejudice in the life of Jonah.
3. Determine the effect of personal prejudices.
4. Resolve to deal with personal prejudices to prevent a breach in their personal relationship with God.

State that the purpose of the study of Jonah's experience is to encourage us to deal with our own prejudices. Invite learners to turn to Jonah 1.

Search for Biblical Truth

Share information about the background of the Book of Jonah found in the introduction of *Studying the Bible*. Display the following outline to guide the study of Jonah 1.

Fleeing from God
Jonah 1—2
I. Jonah's commission (vv. 1-3)
II. Jonah's flight and its consequences (vv. 4-10)
III. A refuge provided (vv. 11-17)
IV. Jonah's prayer from the depths (chap. 2)

Assign each of the passages in the four outline headings to different groups of learners. Direct them to study the assigned section of the Scripture to find answers to the following questions. Provide copies of the questions for the group.

Group 1: Jonah 1:1-3
  1. Why was Jonah directed by God to go to Nineveh?
  2. Why did Jonah buy a ticket instead to Tarshish?
Group 2: Jonah 1:4-10
  1. What was the cause of the great storm?
  2. What caused the seamen to question Jonah about the storm?
  3. How did Jonah respond?
Group 3: Jonah 1:11-17
  1. Why might Jonah be considered a misguided patriot rather than a coward?
  2. What is suggested by the fear and sacrifice of the seamen?
  3. How would you describe the fish that received Jonah?
Group 4: Jonah 2
  1. What new viewpoint does Jonah's prayer suggest?
  2. How did God provide a second chance for Jonah?

Call on learners to report their conclusions to the larger group when they have finished their group study and discussion. When Group 4 discusses Jonah's prayer, share the comments titled "The power of prayer" (*Applying the Lesson*).

Give the Truth a Personal Focus

Ask: Specifically, what was Jonah's major prejudice? (He was prejudiced against the citizens of Nineveh because they were enemies of his people.) How did that prejudice affect his relationship with God? (Note that only when Jonah recognized his prejudice and the disobedience that accompanied it did he have complete fellowship with God.)

Continue by reviewing prejudices acknowledged by learners as the study was begun. Ask: Is it possible that these prejudices are separating us from complete fellowship with God? In what ways do such prejudices keep us from doing what God wants believers to do? Elicit response.

Conclude with a time of meditation and prayer directing learners to come before God acknowledging prejudices they have and asking for wisdom in dealing with them.

---

1. John Bright, *A History of Israel* (Philadelphia: Westminster Press, 1959), 248.
2. Chuck Yeager and Leo Janos, *Yeager* (Toronto: Bantam, 1985), 272.

June 21

Jonah Sulks, and God Saves

Basic Passage: Jonah 3—4

Focal Passages: Jonah 3:1-5,10; 4:1-4,10-11

The Book of Jonah is missions in the Old Testament. Centuries later, the Lord Jesus Christ was to say, "Go ye into all the world, and preach the gospel to every creature" (Mark 16:15). The reluctance of Jonah to obey God's command has had its tragic sequel in the slowness of Christians to share their blessings with others. We are familiar with the obstacles placed in the way of young William Carey when he caught the vision of a world that needed to know of the Savior. A veteran minister rebuked Carey for his enthusiasm and stated that when God was ready to convert the heathen, He would do it Himself, without human aid. The truth is, of course, that God has always been ready, as He was in Jonah's day, but His servants held back from the task. Jonah's story ends with that prophet looking out over Nineveh, with its teeming thousands of people, still unwilling to share the compassion of the Lord for those he regarded as his nation's enemies. Only when the love of God motivates can we engage in redemptive efforts that are effective in reaching people with the gospel of forgiveness and salvation.

Study Aim: *To reexamine the missionary obligation of the church and its members, including ourselves*

STUDYING THE BIBLE

"Jonah was a man in whom piety and duty were ever in conflict; a man who feared God, but at the same time ran away from his task...; a man in whom the spirit of humanity had been almost killed out by patriotism; in short, a man whose religion resided in the realm of emotion, rather than in the sphere of the will. Jesus, in contrast, wept over Jerusalem!"[1]

I. Called a Second Time (Jonah 3:1-4)

Chapters 1 and 3 begin with similar wording, with the exception of one significant clause: "the second time." We might well ask ourselves whether we would have given Jonah another chance to make good. He is not depicted as a pleasant character; though, to give him his due, he does appear in a more attractive light in his witness to the pagan seamen and his willingness to accept death rather than that they all should perish (1:9,12). But this glimpse of another side to his nature only serves to emphasize the depth of his prejudice toward the Ninevites. Once people are branded as enemies it can be hard to regard them in any other light.

> 1 And the word of the Lord came unto Jonah the second time, saying,
>
> 2 Arise, go unto Nineveh, that great city, and preach unto it the preaching that I bid thee.
>
> 3 So Jonah arose, and went unto Nineveh, according to the word of the Lord. Now Nineveh was an exceeding great city of three days' journey.
>
> 4 And Jonah began to enter into the city a day's journey, and he cried, and said, Yet forty days, and Nineveh shall be overthrown.

1. **God's patience (vv. 1-2).**—Jonah had been worse than disobedient; he had tried to "flee . . . from the presence of the Lord" (1:3). There was a spirit of rebellion in his action. Yet, having preserved him from a watery death, the Lord had heeded Jonah when he "prayed unto the Lord his God out of the fish's belly" (2:1). But God's patience with this willful man did not bring release from assignment. Jonah was given a second opportunity to respond to a divine command to go to Nineveh as an appointed messenger. Should we depend on second chances when we willfully reject God's revealed will for our lives?

2. **Jonah's message (vv. 3-4).**—Apparently, Jonah's message was brief and to the point. He was a prophet of doom; yet, from the response of the Ninevites we must assume that what he said carried with it an implication of divine forgiveness. The reference to Nineveh as "an exceeding great city of three days' journey" is difficult to interpret. Many think that a cluster of cities gathered around the capital accounts for the description. We are left to imagine the effect produced by this Israelite prophet stalking through the streets with his message of impending doom, even if it was delivered in what, to the Ninevites, was a foreign tongue.

II. Nineveh Repents (Jonah 3:5-10)

What happened in Nineveh has been offered as an example of the power of preaching. However, the word "preach" (v. 2) can be rendered "proclaim" (NRSV). Jonah's role was more that of a town crier than a preacher. His message, however brief, was nevertheless from

God; therefore, what was unquestionably demonstrated is the effectiveness of a word from the Lord to produce great change. Just as our Lord's sharp command, "Peace, be still" (Mark 4:39), ended the fury of a storm, so Jonah's blunt statement, repeated again and again, produced a response in the Ninevites.

   1. **Popular response** (v. 5).—This began with the people as every level of society decided to take Jonah's message seriously. The depth of their repentance is open to question; but at that time, they acknowledged their sins and, following oriental custom, fasted and dressed themselves in sackcloth.

   2. **Ruler's reaction** (vv. 6-9).—Jonah's message even reached the ears of the ruler of the city, as did also news of the people's demonstration of repentance. The king stripped himself of his royal robes, undoubtedly garments of great splendor, and donned the sackcloth of the people while he also sat on an ash heap. These actions were symbolic of great grief. In his orders to the people, the king referred to their evil ways and "the violence that is in their hands" (v. 8). While Assyria tyrannized neighboring countries, the residents of its capital had engaged in brutalities among themselves. They had plenty for which to repent.

   3. **God's repentance** (v. 10).—The king's call to repentance was made in the hope that it would persuade God to "turn and repent, and turn away from his fierce anger" (v. 9). This expressed hope from a heathen official could not be expected to have the depth of understanding that the idea of a repenting God is given elsewhere in Scripture. But, as the following verse indicates, the command of the king, together with the response of the people, brought about the desired results.

> 10 And God saw their works, that they turned from their evil way; and God repented of the evil, that he had said that he would do unto them; and he did it not.

Human repentance assumes guilt. Yet, with God there is no guilt; so we must look for some other explanation of divine repentance. He does not change in nature or in purpose; but as people change their behavior, so God changes His dealings with them. He is not obligated to carry out His warnings, but He is fully committed to the fulfillment of His promises. Jonah's message of coming judgment was conditional. When Nineveh repented, that judgment was postponed. Jesus also warned of judgment on sin, but He offered forgiveness to the sinner so that this judgment might be escaped. These words of our Lord are memorable: "The men of Nineveh shall rise up in the judgment with this generation, and shall condemn it: for they repented at the preaching of Jonah; and, behold, a greater than Jonah is here" (Luke 11:32).

III. An Angry Prophet (Jonah 4:1-4)

Surely some of the most amazing words in the Bible are in verse 1. Here is a prophet "very angry" because his audience responded to his message, and God accordingly withheld His judgment. In his resentment over being sent to Nineveh, Jonah hoped—even expected—that the people of that city would disregard what he said. When the opposite happened, his indignation was vented on God who had sent him. His prejudices ran so deeply that he could not accept the divine mercy that spared a large city from disaster. The extremes to which deep-rooted prejudice can lead are vividly displayed in Jonah.

> 1 But it displeased Jonah exceedingly, and he was very angry.
> 2 And he prayed unto the Lord, and said, I pray thee, O Lord, was not this my saying, when I was yet in my country? Therefore I fled before unto Tarshish: for I knew that thou art a gracious God, and merciful, slow to anger, and of great kindness, and repentest thee of the evil.
> 3 Therefore now, O Lord, take, I beseech thee, my life from me; for it is better for me to die than to live.
> 4 Then said the Lord, Doest thou well to be angry?

1. **Jonah's desperation (vv. 1-3).**—We see in Jonah a man correct in his understanding of God but devoid of God's Spirit. He was orthodox in belief but erroneous in behavior. In his I-told-you-so prayer, he rightly described the nature of the Lord, which he had learned from personal experience and also from his nation's history. But he did not want these gracious attitudes to be exercised in favor of a foreign people, especially the Assyrians. He felt that he had lost face as a prophet, and he wanted to die.

2. **Time for thought (v. 4).**—Jonah's hasty words produced a mild rebuke from the Lord, "Is it right for you to be angry?" (NRSV). This question was really advice to Jonah to pause and think. What good reason had he for his outburst? What causes lay behind his bitterness? There is no indication that Jonah made any response but continued in his peevish mood.

IV. An Open-Ended Conclusion (Jonah 4:5-11)

Three speechless teachers were used by God in an endeavor to bring Jonah to a better frame of mind. First, God created a fast-growing plant to give Jonah shelter from the sun as he sat watching for the fate of Nineveh. For this, the prophet felt some sense of gratitude, for we read that he "was exceeding glad." Then God allowed a worm to attack the plant so that it died leaving Jonah without shelter. Next God created "a sultry east wind" (NRSV) which caused such physical discomfort that Jonah again wanted to die. Then the Lord spoke to Jonah to show him his foolishness.

> 10 Then said the Lord, Thou hast had pity on the gourd, for the which thou hast not labored, neither madest it grow; which came up in a night, and perished in a night:
> 11 And should not I spare Nineveh, that great city, wherein are more than sixscore thousand persons that cannot discern between their right hand and their left hand; and also much cattle?

"Jonah was concerned over a plant when it was selfishly related to his person; Yahweh was concerned for the inhabitants of a great metropolis"[2] that included 120 thousand persons (NRSV). The prophet was left thinking about this, as should we.

APPLYING THE LESSON

The making of a missionary.—Bill Borden, product of a wealthy home and graduate of Yale and Princeton, did as much for the Lord during his 25 years as many do in a lifetime. He died of meningitis before he could really get to the mission field, but he was a missionary from the moment he became a Christian. One of his Princeton classmates described Bill Borden as "a missionary, first, last and all the time." What produced such a spirit in Bill Borden? One factor was an intense love for God that had been developed through a daily disciplined life. Prayer and Bible study sharpened his insights into God's will. The other factor was a view of the world that came through a round-the-world tour. The trip deepened Bill's understanding of God's love and the need to share that love with the world. Bill Borden returned from the tour with the world on his heart. This tour confirmed his desire to be a missionary. Many of his friends chided him for throwing away his life as a missionary. He simply replied, "You have not seen heathenism." Bill Borden had seen heathenism. More important, he had experienced the love of Christ. This love motivated him to be "a missionary, first, last and all the time."[3]

Jonah was not totally captured by the love of God for the world. Consequently, he did not have the passion for "the heathen" that was demonstrated in Bill Borden's life.

When at first you don't succeed.—A preacher confronted a young man one day who was a part of the drug culture. By his appearance, the young man indicated he had dropped out of society and was on the wrong road. The preacher asked the young man why he had taken this route of radical rebellion. The young man explained he had spent "a whole summer" trying to bring about political and social change in the community he lived in and nothing had come of it. The young man concluded, "I decided that it was hopeless, so I just gave up on life."

Are we not glad that God spent more than "a whole summer" to bring about change in human life? Are we not glad that God does not give up on us the first time we reject Him? The story of Jonah reveals a truth that we see throughout Scriptures: God has infinite patience with human beings. God is the God of the second chance.

The power of God to change.—Manasseh was his name, and evil was his game. He succeeded Hezekiah as king of Judah. Manasseh "practiced witchcraft, used divination, practiced sorcery, and dealt with mediums and spiritists. He did much evil in the sight of the Lord, provoking Him to anger" (2 Chron. 33:6, NASB). Manasseh ignored God until God allowed the king of Assyria to capture him. The Bible explains the change that then came over Manasseh. "And when he was in distress, he entreated the Lord his God and humbled himself greatly before the God of his fathers. When he prayed to Him, He was moved by his entreaty and heard his supplication, and brought him again to Jerusalem to his kingdom. Then Manasseh knew that the Lord was God" (2 Chron. 33:12-13, NASB). After his conversion, Manasseh was a changed person (2 Chron. 33:14-16).

As God changed Manasseh, God also changed the Ninevites. In response to the message of Jonah, they repented and turned to God.

The danger of anger.—Someone has suggested that anger is only one letter away from danger. Winfred Moore quoted a poem that illustrates the spirit of anger:

> Whatever I said in anger,
> Whatever I said in spite;
> I'm sorry I spoke so quickly,
> I thought up some worse ones last night![4]

Jonah could have written that poem. Instead of rejoicing at the repentance of the Ninevites, he regretted it.

One at a time.—Mother Teresa was asked how she could have so much love for the teeming masses of people to whom she ministered. She responded, "I love them one at a time." That could well have been God's answer to Jonah when he questioned God's love for Nineveh. God loved them, as He does us, one at a time.

TEACHING THE CLASS

Main Idea: Our obligation is to share the good news with all persons.

Suggested Teaching Aim: Learners will explain the obligations to share God's message with all persons.

Introduce the Bible Study

Share the comments titled "The making of a missionary" (*Applying the Lesson*). Ask: Who did God intend to be a missionary? Elicit response. Explore the broader meaning of being a missionary, suggesting that all believers are responsible for mission work.

State that God showed Jonah something about who is obligated to do mission work. Note that the purpose for the study today is to help us understand our own role in mission efforts. Invite learners to turn to Jonah 3.

Search for Biblical Truth

Share the quote about Jonah found in the introduction of *Studying the Bible*. Direct learners to look for these characteristics in the Bible passage.

> **A Teaching Outline**
> 1. Consider who is obligated to be a missionary.
> 2. Discover an answer in the experience of Jonah.
> 3. Identify New Testament instructions about missionary efforts.
> 4. Explain personal obligation and the obligation of the church to be involved in missionary effort.

Display the following outline to guide the Bible study.

> A Second Chance—A Second Response
> Jonah 3—4
> I. Called a second time (Jonah 3:1-4)
> II. Nineveh repents (Jonah 3:5-10)
> III. An angry prophet (Jonah 4:1-4)
> IV. An open-ended conclusion (Jonah 4:5-11)

Call on a learner to read Jonah 3:1-4 aloud while others listen to learn of the second call God extended to Jonah to do some missionary work. When the reading is finished, ask questions like these: What does the second call of God to Jonah suggest about God's patience? What did Jonah do when he finally reached Nineveh? Elicit response.

Call on a learner to read Jonah 3:5-10 aloud. Direct other learners to listen to discover how the people of Nineveh responded. Call for response. Note the information from *Studying the Bible* about the oriental customs of the day and the question about the sincerity of the response.

Direct learners to review verse 10. Ask: What is the implication of the statement that God repented? Elicit response. Supplement with information from *Studying the Bible*.

Note the outline heading for the third section. Ask: Why would a speaker be angry when his audience did exactly as he told them to do? State that this is what happened with Jonah. Call on a learner to read

Jonah 4:1-4 aloud. Establish that Jonah's deep-rooted prejudice had not been overcome even though he had been obedient to the direction of God. Note his desperate depression in verse 3. Call attention to verse 4 in which God gently prodded Jonah. Apparently, Jonah continued in his anger.

Call attention to the fourth point on the outline. Note that God continued to try to teach Jonah. He used a vine, a worm, and a sultry east wind. Ultimately, He spoke to Jonah to show him his foolishness. Call on a learner to read Jonah 4:10-11.

When discussing God's second call to Jonah, share the comments titled "When at first you don't succeed" (*Applying the Lesson*). When discussing the repentance of Nineveh, share the comments titled "The power of God to change" (*Applying the Lesson*).

Give the Truth a Personal Focus

Remind learners that the purpose of the study was to determine who is responsible for mission work, that is, for telling others about the way of salvation. Direct learners to spend several minutes discussing the issue with those sitting near them. Direct them to locate Scripture from the New Testament that supports their position. Concordances may be helpful in locating passages. Call for response. Establish through the discussion that every believer has an obligation to mission effort. Ask: In what way are our responses similar to Jonah's? Elicit response.

Share the comments titled "One at a time" (*Applying the Lesson*). Challenge learners to accept their responsibility for mission effort by sharing Jesus with others one at a time.

---

1. George L. Robinson, *The Twelve Minor Prophets* (Grand Rapids: Baker Book House, 1952), 75.
2. A. J. Glaze, Jr., "Jonah" in *The Broadman Bible Commentary*, vol. 7 (Nashville: Broadman Press, 1972), 181.
3. Mrs. Howard Taylor, *Borden of Yale* (Minneapolis: Bethany House Publishers, 1988), 153-54.
4. Winfred Moore, *Faith for the Second Mile* (Nashville: Broadman Press, 1986) 27.

June 28

Judgment and Salvation

Basic Passage: Nahum 1:1—3:19

Focal Passage: Nahum 1:2-3,6-9,12-13,15

Like the Book of Jonah, the prophecy of Nahum is concerned with the city of Nineveh, capital of the Assyrian empire. The former capital had been Assur (Asshur). Nineveh's repentance for its wickedness, as recorded in Jonah, could not have lasted long. There is a probable gap of some 125 years between the respective periods of the two prophecies. Nahum described a condition of abounding evil in what he termed "the bloody city" (3:1), causing God to say, "Behold, I am against thee" (v. 5). So, given an opportunity to renounce its evil past, the people of Nineveh threw away that opportunity and reverted to their former crimes. The severe tone of Nahum must not be allowed to obscure the merciful patience of God who restrained His judgments over a long period of time. He pleaded with Nineveh through that reluctant prophet Jonah, held back His righteous judgment when the people of the city professed repentance, and, after they had revealed a lack of sincerity in this repentance, shielded them from their deserved fate for another century and more. The city fell to the Babylonians and their allies in 612 B.C.

Study Aim: *To give equal weight to what the apostle Paul called "the goodness and severity of God" (Rom. 11:22)*

STUDYING THE BIBLE

God does not settle scores on a weekly basis. While it is ever true that "the wages of sin is death" (Rom. 6:23), those wages are not necessarily paid on Friday night. To quote the title of a famous preacher's sermon, there is a "Payday Some Day." It may be after a short interval, or after the passing of many years, but the justice of God eventually overtakes the sins of individuals and nations.

I. God the Avenger (Nahum 1:2-3)

We know nothing of Nahum beyond what is stated about him in verse 1. Elkosh was apparently his home, a place of uncertain location. His reference to Judah (1:15) encourages the belief that he was a

Judean. The word "burden" describes something "lifted up," hence a proclamation or prophecy to deliver when God's messenger would lift up his hands. The message came to Nahum as a "vision," or revelation. He lost no time in delivering that message.

> 2 God is jealous, and the Lord revengeth; the Lord revengeth, and is furious; the Lord will take vengeance on his adversaries, and he reserveth wrath for his enemies.
>
> 3 The Lord is slow to anger, and great in power, and will not at all acquit the wicked: the Lord hath his way in the whirlwind and in the storm, and the clouds are the dust of his feet.

1. A jealous God (v. 2).—As a human trait, jealousy is often peevish and unreasonable. The word *jealous* occurs frequently in Scripture to describe the Lord's determination to make known His nature and protect that which is His. He does not act rashly, but He acts in justice against His enemies and His people.

2. Restrained power (v. 3).—God's dealings with Nineveh, and the Assyrian empire as a whole, were an example of the truth that He "is slow to anger." God does not give way to temper, as we so often do. His acts of judgment are considered and deliberate. When the time comes for Him to punish sin, He cannot be resisted, for He is "great in power." The second part of verse 3 and following verses declare that His power at work in nature can be made to serve His judgmental purposes.

II. Justice and Mercy (Nahum 1:6-11)

No answers are forthcoming to the questions asked in verse 6, for no answers are necessary. There can be no effective resistance to the judgments of God. If we are surprised at the severity of many of the statements in Nahum, we need to realize that they were addressed to Assyria, represented by its capital: Nineveh. Secular historians have recorded the heinous crimes committed by these people against their enemies. "Woe to the bloody city!" exclaimed Nahum of Nineveh (3:1), a city that bragged of the enormities for which it was guilty, recording them on sculptures made by its own kings.

> 6 Who can stand before his indignation? and who can abide in the fierceness of his anger? his fury is poured out like fire, and the rocks are thrown down by him.
>
> 7 The Lord is good, a stronghold in the day of trouble; and he knoweth them that trust in him.
>
> 8 But with an overrunning flood he will make an utter end of the place thereof, and darkness shall pursue his enemies.
>
> 9 What do ye imagine against the Lord? he will make an utter end: affliction shall not rise up the second time.

1. A contrasted witness (v. 7).—Nahum had earlier spoken a positive word for the Lord, "The Lord is slow to anger" (v. 3). He felt the need to break into the long denunciation of evil and its consequent judgment with another tribute, born out of experience, "The Lord is good" (v. 7). The words sound like a quotation from the Psalms, borrowed by God's prophet as he bore witness to other aspects of His character: His essential goodness, evidenced by His loving care for those who put their trust in Him. Thus even in a judgmental passage of the Old Testament, a note of gospel hope is sounded.

2. Finality of judgment (vv. 8-9).—Returning to the subject of Assyria, its guilt and its doom, the prophet declared the uselessness of trying to escape God's righteous judgments. For the evil empire, the end was in sight. Its destruction would be complete and final. This happened for Nineveh in 612 B.C. All that remains of this famous city are two great mounds of earth. Think of the cities, empires, and dynasties that once dominated the earth but are no more, vanished almost without a trace. Only the record of their atrocities remains to stain the pages of history. Mighty though human forces may be, God can bring them to an "utter end" so that they shall "not rise up the second time."

3. A figure of evil (vv. 10-11).—"From you one has gone out / who plots evil against the Lord, / who counsels wickedness" (v. 11, NRSV). Special mention was reserved for one Assyrian leader whose excesses helped to bring about divine judgment. He is not named, but he might well have been Assurbanipal who boasted of the cruelties he imposed on captured enemies. Almost always when great tyrannies arise, their crimes become concentrated in a single individual, as Hitler and Stalin in our own times. Happily, the opposite is also true, for the grace of God can work through a single person for the benefit of many.

III. Hope for God's People (Nahum 1:12-13)

Destruction of a power such as Assyria was not only an exercise of justice against a tyrant, but also an act of deliverance for those Assyria oppressed, especially God's people Israel.

> 12 Thus saith the Lord; Though they be quiet, and likewise many, yet thus shall they be cut down, when he shall pass through. Though I have afflicted thee, I will afflict thee no more.
> 13 For now will I break his yoke from off thee and will burst thy bonds in sunder.

1. Strength of evil overcome (v. 12a).—We need to change the word "quiet" to "strength," as in the NRSV, to get the meaning here. The power of Assyria is not denied, for there is always danger in underestimating the potential of an enemy. Assyria had the resources and abilities to conquer and subdue surrounding nations, holding them in subjection for long periods. Yet, its military might was powerless against one adversary—namely, God. In their heyday, aggressors may appear invincible and strike terror into all whom they oppose. When confronted by God, they meet their doom.

2. God's instrument (v. 12b).—The second part of verse 12 contains the admission that this fearsome empire had been an instrument in God's hands for the chastisement of His people. "Though I have afflicted thee, I will afflict thee no more." As we will see in a future lesson, God's use of another power (Babylon) to punish His people caused perplexity to the prophet Habakkuk. Yet, in His divine wisdom, this has been a consistent method, used by God throughout history. What may appear to be passing events are the tools in God's hands for imposing penalties and teaching lessons.

3. Deliverance granted (v. 13).—Once again the people Israel were to experience a great deliverance, wrought by the intervention of God. What they could not do for themselves, God did for them, as when He led them out of Egypt. For them, these were experiences of salvation, memorialized in the Passover feast and other festive occasions when they remembered how the Lord had come to their aid. The New Testament writers did not hesitate to see these events as foreshadowings of the great gift of spiritual salvation that came in Christ and is ever available to all who will accept it.

IV. Message of Good Tidings (Nahum 1:15)

Nahum's message, though alarming for Assyria, was good news to the people of Judah who, for a hundred years, had been subjugated to their cruel neighbor in the north. So the prophet assumed a role used by others (Isa. 52:7) as he sounded forth the news of coming deliverance. In days before electronic communications were even dreamed of, runners would carry messages to communities. When they neared the end of their mission, they would mount a nearby hill where they could be seen, and the people were thus prepared to receive information for which they had long waited. The runner became "the feet of him that bringeth good tidings."

> **15 Behold upon the mountains the feet of him that bringeth good tidings, that publisheth peace! O Judah, keep thy solemn feasts, perform thy vows: for the wicked shall no more pass through thee; he is utterly cut off.**

The phrase "good news" becomes "gospel" in the New Testament.

Even so, the defeat and destruction of Assyria becomes for us a symbol of that victory Jesus gained for us over Satan and sin by His death on the cross. The eradication of Israel's enemies foreshadows the time when all that is in opposition to the kingdom of God will meet its end and that kingdom will be revealed in all its glory. For the judgments of God against all that is evil must happen before the eternal reign of Christ and His people begins.

APPLYING THE LESSON

Was it God's judgment?—Jeff Keay lived in Palm Beach Gardens, Florida. This nineteen-year-old man was sitting in his living room with a can of beer in his hand. He later explained that he was listening to a song on the radio entitled, "Your Time Is Going to Come." At that moment, a lightning bolt entered his living room window, discharged through the can of beer in his hand, and sent him to the floor with the force of the jolt. Fortunately, the jolt was not fatal, but it impressed upon him the truth of the song's message for all of us: our time is going to come.[1]

God is a God of infinite patience, but eventually, human sin will be judged by the holiness of God. Nahum's message focused on that judgment side of God.

Evidences of a hard heart.—The problem in Nahum's day, as in our day, is that too many people had hardened their hearts toward God. What are some of the marks of a hard heart? This is the answer given by Warren Wiersbe: "An unwillingness to admit and confess my own sins. A bitter spirit toward another believer. An unwillingness to forgive. A resistance to the Word of God. An inflexible attitude that cannot be taught or changed. A feeling that my way is the right way and the only way. A fear of change and an unwillingness to learn new things. A refusal to let people get 'too close.' A touchiness of spirit, a supersensitive attitude that makes it difficult for people to get along with me. Being preoccupied with my own needs and not being concerned about the needs of others."[2]

Whenever these tendencies are present in our lives, we need to hear again the word of warning from God's prophet, for they are clear evidences of a hard heart.

How the mighty are fallen.—At times, perpetrators of sin appear to be invincible. Yet, as time passes, evil people and evil nations inevitably are destroyed by the consequences of their own sins.

Al Capone is a good example. That name is familiar with most Americans, even today, for it epitomized the power evil men wielded over the lives of other people. He operated out of a suite at the Hotel Lexington on Michigan Avenue in Chicago. In his prime, he ruled over a thousand men and grossed more than $100 million a year through his gambling, prostitution rings, and bootlegging. He squelched every opponent. He controlled the crime world of his day. How invincible Capone seemed to be.

And how he eventually fell! He was indicted for income tax evasion, convicted, and sent to a federal penitentiary. His medical exam revealed that he had syphilis. After several years in prison, he was found one day in 1938, staring blankly into space. He was in the final stages of syphilis. His last eleven months in prison were spent in a hospital ward; and then when released, he retired to his Palm Island estate in Florida. There he continued to lose his mind. His speech became garbled, and his mind was confused. He died on January 25, 1947, of a brain hemorrhage. The death of this man who once controlled the city of Chicago and ruled over a thousand men was reported on page seven of the newspaper. How the mighty are fallen!

Nineveh had that same air of invincibility when Nahum pronounced his message. Yet, they too would fall, victim to the consequences of their own sins.

What was God doing?—All night long the little girl trembled in her bed at the sound of the thunder. It was the worst storm she had ever known. The next morning she asked her father, "What was God doing last night during the storm?" Before the father could respond, however, she answered her own question. She said, "I know. God was making the morning."

The Israelites may have wondered where God was during the oppression they suffered under the Assyrians. The prophet Nahum answered their question: "God was making the morning."

The lessons we learn from suffering.—Alexander Solzhenitsyn described how his suffering actually led him to God. He wrote, "It was only when I lay there on rotting prison straw that I sensed within myself the first stirrings of good. . . . So, bless you, prison, for having been in my life."

In a similar way, the prophet Nahum declared to the Israelites that good things would come out of their suffering under the Assyrians.

TEACHING THE CLASS

Main Idea: Ultimately God must punish evil.

Suggested Teaching Aim: Learners will respond to the fact that ultimately God must punish evil.

Introduce the Bible Study

Write *Nahum* on the chalkboard. Ask: Do you recall what the Book of Nahum is about? Elicit response. Use information from the introductory comments to the lesson to provide information.

Write the main idea on the chalkboard. Note that while God is patient and long-suffering, there is no doubt on the basis of the Scripture that the main idea is true. State that the purpose of the study is to help us to come to grips with the fact that God must punish evil, not only in the lives of the minorities but in our own lives as well. Invite learners to open their Bibles to Nahum 1.

Search for Biblical Truth

Display the following outline to guide the Bible study.

> Judgment and Salvation
> I. God, the avenger (Nah. 1:2-3)
> II. God, just and merciful (Nah. 1:6-11)
> III. God, provider of hope for His people (Nah. 1:12-13)
> IV. God, messenger with good tidings (Nah. 1:15)

Call on a learner to read Nahum 1:2-3 aloud. Call attention to section 1 of the outline. Ask: What words or phrases in this passage support the truth that God is an avenger and that He must ultimately punish evil?

A Teaching Outline
1. Focus on the inevitability of judgment.
2. Discover how God ultimately judged Nineveh.
3. Determine evidence of evil in our own lives that must ultimately be punished.
4. Respond personally to the fact that God will ultimately punish evil.

Share the comments titled "Was it God's judgment?" (*Applying the Lesson*). Ask: How is the judgment of God brought into our own lives? Establish that much of our behavior has its own negative results that is used by God to bring judgment on our lives.

Share the comments titled "Evidences of a hard heart" (*Applying the Lesson*). Suggest that God's judgment on a hard heart is severe. Encourage learners to evaluate their own hearts.

Note that while God must judge evil because of who He is, He also offers justice and mercy because of who He is. Call on a learner to read verses 6-9 aloud. When the reading is finished, ask: What is the only hope against the justice of God? (His mercy is the only hope.)

Call on a learner to read verses 12-13 while other learners listen for the statement of mercy and provision of hope for God's people. Ask again: What is the source of deliverance from the judgment of God? Note verse 13. God will break the yoke of sin and grant deliverance.

Share the comments titled "What was God doing?" (*Applying the Lesson*). Note that God is always working toward a way of bringing redemption to those who turn to Him. The final verse for study sings out the joyful news that the message of salvation is from God. Call on a learner to read Nahum 1:15 aloud.

Give the Truth a Personal Focus

Ask rhetorically: Is it possible that there is sin in our own lives that God must ultimately punish? Will He punish that sin even if we are redeemed by the blood of Jesus? Remind learners that God's nature makes it impossible for Him not to avenge evil. Continue by asking further: What response do we need to make personally in view of the fact that God must punish evil?

Share the comments titled "The lessons we learn from suffering" (*Applying the Lesson*). Invite learners to spend a few moments in prayer responding to God on the basis of the fact that He must ultimately punish evil.

---

1. *Pensacola News-Journal*, 9 July 1985, 1a.
2. Warren Wiersbe, *Real Worship* (Nashville: Oliver Nelson, 1986), 105-06.
3. Charles R. Swindoll, *Encourage Me* (Portland: Multnomah Press, 1982), 43.